Leaving Trump America

To Live the American Dream

Robert McClellan

Dedication

To the remarkable Jill Heinerth,
the love of my life, and reason
I awake each day with a smile in Canada.

Table of Contents

Introduction

"It's no measure of health to be well adjusted to a profoundly sick society" -- J. Krishnamurti

I am the person. I did it.

A lot of people declared they would leave America if Donald Trump were elected president. There was a whole group of screeching celebrities who promised they'd pick up and move if Trump beat Hillary Clinton. They howled at the moon and swore into the night that they would leave America if he took the oath of office on January 20, 2017.

Me too.

To the best of my knowledge, most of these A-List folks still live in New York, Connecticut, California, and New Jersey.

In America.

Okay, I'm not even a "D-Lister" and can hardly get a check cashed at our bank without my wife there to vouch for me, but, I did it.

I left America.

I didn't curse or howl as much, but I did get to the point where I was uncomfortable in my own country. I began to see many similarities to what was currently happening in America and the events in Europe of the 1930s.

During the 2016 campaign, I found out I had north Florida neighbors who were orgasmic with the possibility of "The Donald" in the Oval Office. Many of these neighbors now consider me a former friend.

A year into MAGA hell, when the dust settled, and the social, economic and political reality of life in the United States under a Trump regime became apparent, I left Florida and moved to Canada.

I predict there will be many following behind me. Legal cannabis and a functional parliamentary democracy with a social safety net may prove too big a temptation for a lot of Americans who have the means to get here. Yes, it gets cold, but I've learned that Tim Horton's coffee and local kids playing ice hockey at the community arena help make the Canadian winters tolerable. I moved to a small Ontario town in January while the province was experiencing record low temperatures and my eyeballs froze in their sockets. With Jill, my Canadian wife, I bought a small condo in a renovated two-hundred-year-old mill on a cascading river about thirty minutes outside of Ottawa. A year later, America looks much different from here.

Today, the Trump Administration has taken a strange course. Many well-known pop-culture and political personalities have pledged allegiance to a loosely defined movement called "The Resistance." But hashtags on Twitter and rants on Facebook have done little to stop Trump's shredding the Constitution and steamrolling the Rule of Law.

I had vehemently opposed Trump's presidency from the moment I saw the footage of him gliding down that ridiculous escalator announcing his presidential campaign. Every time I see that footage I get nauseous. He looks like the latest Bond villain surveying his lair. My coping mechanism is to imagine him descending slowly into the depths of hell.

Hey America! How did we fall for such a con-man? Why didn't we send him right back up the other side of the escalator, never to be taken seriously again?

Oh, because we were pissed off at the establishment, and he promised to protect jobs, build a wall, lock up Hillary, and "Make America Great Again."

How's that workin' out?

Yep. I did it. I'm the guy. I'm the one who left Donald Trump's America.

I Love America

I love America. I love Americans. I am an American, and no matter where I choose to live, I will always be. But, I am an empath, and the harm I see America inflicting upon itself hurts me. It is as though the country is made up of 327 million cutters, slashing at their arms so they can feel…anything. The warm blood trickles over their wrists and drips onto the floor between their overpriced Air Jordan's and glittering ruby slippers.

The shady cabal that controls America loves the fact that Americans are dysfunctional and self-destructive. As we tear at each other's throats based on political persuasion, race, religion, and culture, the American oligarchs are on their mega-yachts, smoking Cuban cigars and sipping Russian Vodka, laughing all the way to their Cayman Islands banks.

America is a nation in crisis. While the Alt-right and Progressive left are busy killing each other on the streets of Charlottesville, our overlords are using drugs, sports, booze, and sex to distract the rest of us while they dismantle the constitutional republic our founders drafted in 1787 at Independence Hall. As long as we have Facebook, Netflix, and the NFL, we seem content to apathetically drift further apart from each other. Our smartphones dumb us down, and our social media makes us anti-social. We retreat into the echo chambers of our safe spaces whenever we encounter opposing points of view, plugging in wireless earbuds to drown out the cacophony of real life.

My version of the American Dream wasn't supposed to be like this.

I was raised to believe anything was possible. My potential was limitless, and I was infinitely optimistic. If I worked hard, I was promised a peaceful and creative world, where socio-economic classes, sex, race, and religion were antiquated stereotypes from a more vulgar time. Using technology and science, I'd evolve with a new enlightenment—a silicon-based spirituality. However, my naive expectations collided with early 21st-century reality, and it was not so much a dream, as a nightmare. My middle-aged life in America wasn't supposed to be like this. This hard, mean, fearful, corrupt, and greedy.

We American men can be dark and self-defeating, sabotaging our happiness. The light of our expectations has dimmed. We were born into the most prosperous and dynamic generation in history, then pissed away our potential.

Our superficial Baby Boomer mantra is "he who dies with the most toys wins." To this end, we shine custom chromed Harley's in three-car garages while our post-menopausal wives open the mail and find another overdue credit card bill. Now, in our graying years, we groan as Wrangler waistlines expand and 401K balances contract. We medicate our sallow-skinned children into submission and anesthetize our unfulfilled American dreams with Xanax and craft-brewed beers.

It wasn't supposed to be like this.

You have seen us around. Marching like lemmings into big box home centers, we try to connect with our self-reliant ancestry. We use the inherited hand-tools with which our grandfather's built their own houses, but need a laser level smartphone app to hang a picture frame in our daughter's bedroom.

We are the sons of the "Greatest Generation." Our parents built the most advanced and prosperous society in history. And they gave it to us.

Born after the Second World War, and coming of age in the "Happy Days" of the nineteen fifties and sixties, we Boomers were baptized in the holy waters of optimism.

We landed a man on the moon and invented the Internet. We discovered Ray Charles and birthed the Beatles. Together, we fought for civil rights and elected the first Black president. Dutifully, we went to Vietnam, Bosnia, and Desert Storm. Today, we patriotically send our kids to the military quagmires of Iraq and Afghanistan. We cheered as the U.S.A. Hockey team won Olympic gold; and in the arms of strangers, we cried in horror as the Twin Towers fell.

We are simultaneously the best and the worst that America produces. An enigma enveloped in a generational contradiction. We build and destroy with impunity. On our way to meet our buddies at the sports bar, we callously step around the homeless man, not considering that we may be only a few drinks away from the same fate.

For our penance, on weekends take our kids to soccer and ice cream and continue the farce that all is well in our little deed-restricted world.

It wasn't supposed to be like this.

Just a few short decades ago, America was the shining light of the world. Americans were the most well-educated, innovative, healthy, and prosperous people on the planet. Now, at the twilight's last gleaming, the United States is slipping in almost every area that measures a nation's well being. In healthcare, education, and quality of life, America has declined from consistently near the top of the ratings, down to the high teens to mid-twentieth places when compared to other modern countries. But still, we hear the chants of "We're Number One!" and "U.S.A., U.S.A.!" from a brainwashed populace still holding on to the notion that we are the greatest at damn near everything. (We reluctantly concede that Canada will always be better at ice hockey and curling). While the United States outspends everyone on healthcare and education, the results are disappointing. Throwing money at problems doesn't usually solve them. From my own anecdotal experience, I see large parts of American society that are illiterate, barely able to read the BOGO special labels at the local dollar store. How many times have you confused a young cashier when you offered extra coins at the cash register to facilitate receiving only paper bills as your change? They struggle with the concept of math and usually have to consult a manager. These are young people who are in high school, tenth graders who can't count or read. That's why they are so comfortable with the visual mediums of YouTube and Instagram. No text required.

This concept of "American Exceptionalism" was never based on reality. It was just another mind fuck perpetrated on an unsuspecting public mollifying them into approving the never-ending wars and conflicts the Corporate Masters needed to pad their military-industrial investment portfolios. Brainwashing the masses into believing that we are spreading our highly superior democratic American values around the world via military force, allows them to run roughshod over resource-rich nations with corrupt leaders and no significant military opposition.

America is eating itself from the inside. There is a cancer growing in our society. Everyone is pointing the fingers of blame for the unhealthy state in which we find ourselves. This diagnosis was made a long time ago by people much smarter than me. Dwight D. Eisenhower warned us about the unchecked power of a military-industrial complex. (Ike was president in 1957, the year I was born). In the 70s' we saw the whole Watergate fiasco, where a sitting president was a principal part of a botched political crime and cover-up. The lessons from Watergate loom large today, but the current Congress cannot get beyond political partisanship to do their constitutional duty.

I love America but, man, what a hot mess she is right now.

But there is hope. America can recover.

The first step is to admit there is a problem - and no, the problem does not live at 1600 Pennsylvania Avenue. The problem lives in Missouri, North Dakota, Florida, California...every single state, city, town, and county in America.

The problem is us.

"Us" as in "We The People," stood apathetically on the sidelines as a pack of grifters hijacked our country's wealth, institutions and most of our government. We drifted into an orgasm of consumerism and affluence, busy getting new tattoos and shining our bass boats while a group of well-financed political and corporate hacks stole our country from us.

When I say "We The People," I mean all of us. Republicans, Democrats, Liberals, Conservatives, Christians, Buddhists, Muslims, Agnostics, Atheists and Jews. All of us who work for a living. All of us who are not the 1%. No matter our beliefs, our sexual preference or skin color, we must come together and save America. If we don't, we will find our country permanently in the hands of oligarchs, dictators, and authoritarians with no respect for anything except their wealth and power. I know this sounds dramatic, but these are extraordinary times. Every single world power in history has been brought to its knees by either conquest or corruption. The United States is in no immediate danger of being conquered militarily. However, we are precariously close to losing our democracy to corrupt internal forces who have no allegiance to anything beyond raw power.

With the limited release of the redacted Mueller Report to the Congress and the actions of an Attorney General who is acting more like a mob lawyer to the president rather than the nation's highest ranking law enforcement officer, I hope some eyes have opened to the real and present dangers our country faces.

Rather than arguing with each other on Internet forums and Twitter, we should be marching by the millions on Washington, demanding to see the entire, un-redacted report. Instead of gluing ourselves to the final episodes of "Game of Thrones," or staying up late to see the NBA Finals, we should be out in our communities helping young people to register to vote.

We are at a critical point in history. A lot of my militia friends like to say, "by the ballot box or by the bullet box, We the People will prevail." I've always believed that the ballot is the most potent weapon in our arsenal. But some are itching for trouble, hoping the current political chaos leads to violence.

I think we have one more chance.

This is it.

If We the People do not exercise our responsibilities and vote for the type of leadership we deserve, we are lost.

If you look at most of the independent polling and responsible journalism in America right now, it doesn't look like Donald Trump has a chance to win re-election. I'd like to believe this is accurate. And yet, we must consider that the Russian wild card will be in play for the 2020 election. As far as Robert Mueller and I can tell, the Russians interfered with the 2016 election and have every intention of doing so again. It also is becoming painfully apparent that few, if any, federal agencies are trying to prevent this meddling. And, I don't think Trump will voluntarily leave office, even if he loses.

Then, all hell will break loose.

Just the fact that serious pundits and policy wonks are discussing this scenario is frightening. I can't find a single moment in our nation's history where the peaceful transfer of power was ever in doubt.

There is one way to assure that Donald John Trump is a one-term president who will, however reluctantly, concede power. That is to vote so overwhelmingly for his Democratic opponent that even Trump gets the message through his thick, combed-over skull. If the election results show a landslide against Trump, his handlers and puppet-masters will have to relinquish the White House. They won't go easily and maybe not without a fight. But, if the vote totals show him losing by significant margins, even the Trump-stacked Supreme Court would have no basis to support his unconstitutional claim to the throne.

The Turning Point

In January of 2017, I hit a milestone, my 60th birthday. As a prank gift, my fellow Americans gave me Donald Trump as President. It was the worst present since I got soap on a rope in grade seven. As I watched Trump being sworn in, I secretly wished I had a long noose of soapy rope to relieve my misery.

I was born when Dwight D. Eisenhower was President. He graduated from West Point, had a distinguished military career, culminating as Supreme Commander of Allied Forces during the WWII. Donald Trump received a medical diagnosis of bone spurs from a doctor who was his father's tenant. Based on this dubious condition, Trump was given a deferment from the Vietnam draft. I served nine years on active duty in the U.S. military. I went to boot camp with guys from Appalachia who spent most of their young lives running barefoot across rocks. They had far worse podiatry issues than "bone spurs." Day one of boot camp was the first time they owned a proper pair of lace-up leather shoes. Many of these men, who came from the poorest counties in

America, went on to serve honorably for twenty years or more. Some of them, I'm sure, made the ultimate sacrifice for their country in the Persian Gulf. Bone spurs, my ass!

Cowardice, coupled with rich white boy entitlement, is the only debilitating affliction from which Donald Trump suffered in the Vietnam era. I don't care how many times he wraps himself in the flag, (yes, that's a thing he actually does), he doesn't fool many veterans with his hollow patriotism. He, nor any of his children, have ever served a single minute in the military. Genealogical researchers have perused 150 years of records, including Trump's ancestors in Kallstadt, Germany, and cannot find a single Trump who served in the military. It is reported that Donald Trump's grandfather, Friedrick Trump, emigrated in 1885 from Bavaria to the United States. According to Bavarian records, this emigration was illegal, as, at the age of 16, the young Mr. Trump was required to, but had not yet served his mandatory two years in military service to the Bavarian Kingdom. I'm sensing a trend here.

Donald Trump's supporters like to point to a photo of him as a young man in a cadet uniform. The fact is, for a short time, he was a student at a military-themed boarding school and like every other enrolled student, was a member of the campus ROTC (Reserve Officer Training Corps). It would be like a Boy Scout trying to pass for a Green Beret, wearing similar uniforms, but worlds apart.

I'm not saying that military service should be a prerequisite for the presidency, though most of the presidents of my lifetime have at one time worn the uniform. Every President from Harry Truman to George H.W. Bush served. Even Richard Nixon was in the Navy, for fuck's sake. He was a Commander in the Pacific during the Second World War, and his unit earned two battle stars. Trump's predecessor, Barack Obama did not serve, nor did Bill Clinton. But neither of these men appointed themselves as the ultimate arbiter of American patriotism. When Donald Trump questions the patriotism of and threatens NFL players who kneel in protest during the national anthem, he defiles the office of the presidency and proves he knows nothing of the Black American struggle or the Bill of Rights. Even more grievously, he demonstrates his ignorance to the men and women of the Armed Forces of every race, color, and creed who, even today, sacrifice everything so that we may all enjoy these Rights.

As a disabled veteran, I depend on the Veterans Medical Centers (the V.A.) for my primary healthcare. I and many of my fellow veterans would like the V.A. to be a dependable agency that meets the needs of all veterans.

President Trump's first V.A. secretary was David Shulkin, the first non-veteran named to the position. At least he was a physician. But, it is rumored that Trump fired Shulkin after just a year in the job because he resisted Administration efforts to privatize V.A. healthcare. After dismissing Shulkin, Donald Trump named his personal White House doctor, Ronny Jackson to head the agency. The world met Doctor Jackson when he stepped up to the podium and gushed that the President was in excellent health for this term and, by the way, a second. Jackson allegedly lied about Trump's weight and cognitive state. Dr. Jackson was never confirmed by the Senate and withdrew his nomination after it was alleged that he drinks during work hours and liberally hands out benzodiazepines, opioids, and other controlled drugs to Trump staffers. Montana Senator Jon Testor told CNN that the White House staff referred to Jackson as "The Candy Man."

But, again speaking as a veteran, the point where my suspicion and dislike of Trump turned to pure disdain was when, during the presidential campaign, he attacked the Khan family.

You may recall that Khizr and Ghazala Khan are Pakistani-Americans whose son, Army Captain Humayun Khan was killed-in-action in Iraq in 2004. He was twenty-seven years old and according to Army accounts, died while protecting his troops when a car bomb rolled up to them. During the Democratic National Convention, the Khans appeared together on stage in front of massive picture of their deceased son. Mr. Khan called then-candidate Trump out on several issues, most notably his proposed ban on immigration from Muslim majority countries. In a blistering, emotional speech, Mr. Khan, a Harvard-trained lawyer by profession, held up a pocket-sized copy of the United States Constitution and proclaimed:

"Donald Trump, you're asking Americans to trust you with their future. Let me ask you, have you even read the United States Constitution? I will gladly lend you my copy. In this document, look for the words "liberty" and "equal protection of law…""

"Have you ever been to Arlington Cemetery? Go look at the graves of brave patriots who died defending the United States of America. You will see all faiths, genders, and ethnicities. You have sacrificed nothing—and no one."

Mr. Khan's son, Captain Humayun Khan is buried at Arlington.

Donald Trump went immediately into attack mode. He accused the Khans' of being puppets of Hillary Clinton, and that Clinton's campaign staff wrote the speech. Mr. Khan insisted he wrote the address himself and the part where he held up the Constitution was wholly ad-libbed and spur of the moment. In true Trump fashion, the future President then attacked Mrs. Khan, criticizing her presence on the stage, implying a connection between her silence and Islamic gender roles. Here is Trump's direct quote, from his ABC News interview with George Stephanopoulos:

"If you look at his wife, she was standing there. She had nothing to say. She probably, maybe she wasn't allowed to have anything to say. You tell me." (It must be a grueling task for journalists to transcribe Trump's "word salad" speech patterns.) As Melania Trump stands silently beside Donald on most occasions, I guess the irony is lost on him.

Ghazala Khan later revealed that she had planned to speak, but was so overcome with emotion after seeing the picture of her son that she could not, and asked her husband to speak for the whole family.

Trump then went on to say he also made a lot of sacrifices and built "great structures," crowing "I've had tremendous success."

I was home in Florida that night, in bed with Jill, my Canadian wife, watching Khan's speech. It brought tears to both our eyes. Afterward, in what may prove to be my least prescient moment, through my snot and blubbering, I said, "well, it looks like Hillary just won the election."

The next day, watching Trump's response to the Khan family brought rage to every nerve in my body. If there is one thing, one subject that is sacred to me, it is military service. Unless you've been there, unless you've raised your hand and taken that oath, a promise that you might have to back up with your very life, you may not understand. I'm not "America first, red, white and patriotic blue." I know America is an imperfect and incomplete experiment. But, what I can't accept is a coward, in a position of power, that exploits military members and veterans for selfish political gain. And to question the motives of a Gold Star mother, no matter where she was born or what religion she chooses, as an image of her hero son is splashed on a screen behind her, is not only cowardice, I'd say it borders on sociopathy.

I am a Baby Boomer. When I was born in 1957, America was the envy of the world. I am fortunate to have come into this life when my country enjoyed great prosperity. My parents experienced WWII and scraped together a modest living in Philadelphia. My dad joined the Army Air Corps near the conclusion of the war, and in 1947 was one of the first enlisted men to become a member of the fledgling U.S. Air Force. He never saw combat but was involved in weapons testing in the Nevada desert. I've often wondered if exposure to those atomic tests led to his early death from leukemia.

We Boomers were naturally optimistic. The sky was our limit, and we proved it by putting men on the moon and rovers on Mars. We went on to build the most advanced and prosperous society in history. We created marvelous technology like smartphones, and are on the verge of developing artificial intelligence capable of performing beyond our wildest dreams. But, despite our intellectual achievements, we can't seem to get a handle on poverty, injustice, or racism. We lit a spark of equality during the sixties, and forty years later went on to elect the first African-American President. But as they say, "two steps forward, one step back." The election of Donald Trump is less like a giant leap for humanity than it is a clumsy slog through the swampy marsh of the deplorable mess our society has become.

During the 2016 presidential campaign, like millions of other Americans, I never thought Donald Trump could win the election. And, based on the total vote count, he did not. Hillary Clinton won the popular vote by about three million. But, because the United States still uses the electoral college voting system from the mid-nineteenth century, Trump prevailed. Yes, in this age of global digital literacy and the secure Blockchain, we still use a presidential election process devised 175 years ago by horse-riding, land-owning white men, who prohibited women from voting and wrote into law that African-Americans are 3/5th of a person. Chew on that for a while.

Recently, my Canadian father-in-law invited me to the men's' coffee club at his church, where I might help explain the U.S. electoral college to a group of mostly 80-something-year-old guys. I researched it a bit, lazily reading the Electoral College Wikipedia page, and prefaced my talk with a caveat. I said, "even real college professors who teach actual political science in real universities struggle with understanding the electoral college. I'm just some knucklehead American guy with an Internet connection and Google, but I'll give it the old electoral college try." Some of them got the joke. The hardest point to make clear to these fine gentlemen was how the candidate with the lowest total of popular votes was, in the end, elected. We were on the Electoral College Bowl twenty yard line, and a difficult hour later, wouldn't move much further down the field. These guys were not some radical political action group. These were nice guys, Toronto neighbors who had successful careers, raised their families, and retired comfortably. They possessed that defining Canadian character trait: an innate sense of fair play. In their world, the Stanley Cup goes to the team that wins the best four-out-of-seven playoff hockey games. The Grey Cup goes to the Canadian football team with the most points on the board at the end of the CFL championship game.

I leaned on all my Toastmaster's public speaking skills during my presentation, and I think some of the coffee club finally understood. Our American election system was exposed as less than perfect in the 2000 election when the hanging chad debacle gave us George W. Bush over Al Gore. (Vice-President Gore also received more of the popular vote). Sixteen years later we were utterly fucked when Trump, who received millions of fewer votes than Clinton, was declared the winner. There were some coffee club guys with extreme, anti-Trump opinions, based on a lot of the same morality as their liberal-American cousins. Some others weren't concerned with Trump's blatant misogyny or racism. They were more upset with the concept of unfairness. They muttered, "How can the person with the most votes lose…?" It seemed to me the men were highly disappointed in America. The Canadians I know and love are very aware and concerned about what happens south of their border. Not in a "build that northern wall" way, but more like "Geez, sorry…we hope you guys are okay down there…is there anything we can do to help?" I suspect that as things have played out for Canada so far with this Trump administration, a lot of these Snowbird retirees may not be wintering in Florida or Arizona anytime soon. We know a handful of Canadian friends who are taking their vacations in Mexico rather than Florida. When pressed, they admit that their decisions are influenced by Trump's antagonistic attitude toward Canada and Prime Minister Justin Trudeau.

Like millions of other Americans, I became mesmerized by the media juggernaut that was Donald Trump's presidential campaign. I never watched an episode of his "The Apprentice" reality T.V. show, but I didn't miss a debate and tuned in to many of his interviews. Say what you will about Trump, but he is a narcissistic media genius. His entire career was built on drawing attention to himself and his projects, and now, this campaign was his most significant project of all.

I can't remember seeing a single paid Donald Trump campaign ad, but it seemed that all the news organizations were going balls-to-the-wall with 24/7 Trump coverage.

Early on, as he stood on the debate stages, surrounded by his stuffed shirt Establishment Republican rivals, I couldn't wait to hear what outrageous thing he'd say next. With his practice of juvenile name-calling - "Little Marco" for Rubio, or "Lyin' Ted" for Cruz, Trump managed to bring all his rivals down to the New York back alley level of politics he knew he could win. These GOP stalwarts, from sitting U.S. Senators, to state Governors and successful business icons, they all took his bait. He reeled them in like helpless blowfish, making them look like weak and pathetic candidates. The biggest mistake each one of them made was not taking Donald J. Trump seriously. He doesn't like to lose. Underestimate him at your peril.

I'd sit with Jill and watch the debates like I was watching a sporting event. Trump turned the traditionally civil, yet dull T.V. debates into a blood sport. The Republican debates were beginning to look like a WWE wrestling cage match, and only one gladiator would be left standing at the end of each episode. After each debate, fewer contestants were remaining in the arena. He was starting to hand some of the country club GOP candidates their asses. Jeb Bush, who I liked and voted for as Florida governor, was particularly flabbergasted. I was developing a grudging admiration of Trump for the way he defeated his foes. I once said to my wife, "At least he's shaking up the Establishment. They need someone to come in and bring them back to reality. Maybe he's the right guy at the right time." She threatened to divorce me on the spot if I ever uttered such nonsense again. But, I did secretly like the way he disrespected the rules and was reinventing the political game. He made mince meat out of the GOP Establishment and claimed his crown in Cleveland with all the humility of a golden demigod emperor. It was good T.V.

But, now he had to face the full wrath of one of the most powerful political machines on earth: The Clintons.

Jill and I were lukewarm Hillary Clinton supporters. We both voted for Bernie Sanders in the Democratic Primary. We were little progressive fish living in a large conservative pond. During the 2016 election season, our small Florida county's registration numbers were two-thirds Republican with the rest mostly Democrats, some Libertarians, and a few exciting others like the Peg-legged Pirate Party that for some reason wasn't taken seriously. In Florida, a voter must belong to one of the two major parties if they want to vote in the Democratic or Republican primary elections to select the candidate who will run in the general election. In recent years I've bounced back and forth from Democrat to "no party affiliation." I come from a solid Democrat family, with trade union roots. During the 2016 Democratic primary, Jill persuaded me to place a Bernie Sanders lawn sign next to our mailbox along the county road. It was a half-mile walk from the mailbox to our front door. After the sign appeared, many of our conservative Christian neighbors shunned us. Thank goodness. I can only take so many, "Have a blessed days" in one lifetime. Some of my guy friends chalked it up to my wife's influence that was hatched in her frozen socialist homeland of Canada. They said, "Hey Rob, we understand. Just do whatever you need to keep peace with the wife." I hate when men use that term. It reveals a lot about their misogynistic character. If you refer to your loving life partner as, "The Wife," then, fuck off, please. "Brah."

Surprisingly, the Bernie Sanders sign stayed in place for about a week. Then, one afternoon, I went down to get the mail, and it was gone. Not smashed, knocked over, or vandalized. It just disappeared. In the county where we lived on a rural two-lane road, I was expecting to see the Bernie sign blown to pieces by 12-gauge buckshot. Nope. Just poof! Gone. It couldn't possibly have been Hillary's people. There was no Clinton campaign office in our county or any of the neighboring communities.

We saw zero Hillary Clinton lawn signs in our area during the entire primary campaign. Only a few popped up during the general election, but never on a person's lawn or property. They'd be at state road intersections - at least until Joe Bob, Dwayne and his other brother Travis ran them over with their diesel, coal-rollin' pickup trucks. A Hillary Clinton sign had a very short life span in north-central Florida. The Democrats didn't even bother opening a northern Florida headquarters. What was the point? They knew they'd win the progressive oasis of Alachua County and Gainesville, where the University of Florida was located. On the political party affiliation map, Gainesville looks like a blue island surrounded in a sea of red. North Florida is a GOP stronghold. God, guns, and gays are the topics of political discourse. Any candidate that wants to win at any level, from Sheriff to Congress, must adopt these themes across Gilchrist, Marion, Columbia, Levy, Dixie, Hamilton, Suwannee, Union, Baker, Clay, Putnam and Duval counties. And, they must belong to an evangelical church. There are little country churches every few miles along the roads of North Florida. It is truly the buckle of the Bible Belt.

When Primary Election Day arrived in 2016, we voted at the quaint Gilchrist County Community Center three miles down the road from our house. As middle-class white people, we had no problem getting a ballot. I don't understand all the rhetoric about "voter I.D." Every time I've voted, in Pennsylvania, South Dakota, or Florida, I've always had to provide identification. We handed our driver's licenses over to the pleasant woman behind the desk, and she gave us our ballots, along with the little plastic privacy folder we used to feed the completed ballots into the tally machine. I think we caught her a little off guard when she looked up our registration on the voting rolls and saw a big "D" next to our names. I hovered over her desk as she used a 12-inch ruler to skim down the long page to find my name. Rep-Rep-Rep-Rep-Rep-Rep-Rep-Dem. Yea! "Dem." That's me. "Oh, ya'll are going to need a Democratic ballot," she said quietly as she peeled them off a short pile and placed them in the folders. It was almost as if she didn't want to reveal our political perversion to anyone within earshot. She said, "Democrat" just like some people stage-whisper "Cancer." Oh, sorry to hear about your political "cancer."

The next day, the county website posted the Primary voting results. The raw numbers are made public, but not the identities of the voters. They are broken down by precinct and polling location. At our little community center, there were only 18 democratic votes cast. Four went to Sanders and the rest to Clinton. We made it our mission to find the other two Sanders' voters. We'd definitely like to have them over for dinner and intelligent conversation. A few weeks passed and my wife ran into our friends, a couple who recently moved down from Chicago. They are both involved in live theater production and are officers of IATSE, the largest stagehand's union in the country. Yep. They were the other two Bernie votes! We finally had dinner with them in December. (Dinner and tears, as it was after Trump won the general election.)

Well, the primary went Hillary's way, even if distorted by some "Bernie Bro" antics at the DNC convention. Everyone knew it would be Hillary's coronation. We recognized that she was more than qualified for the position, and I found myself looking forward to voting for the first woman President of the United States. Not surprisingly, my ultraconservative neighbors hopped aboard the Trump train. Where it was going, none could say, all they knew was that he hated "the Muzzies," would build a Mexican wall, and was going to Make America Great Again. Trump campaign signs popped up all over the place.

Some people even strung hand-made Trump banners and lighted placards on the sides of sheds and barns. Trump struck a chord with these folks. Unfortunately, some of these people were my well-armed, right-wing fanatic neighbors. I thought I knew them. I lived among them for a dozen years. Some, I'd consider good friends. But, like everything Trump touches, many relationships turned to shit over his election. Families fought over it, friendships were strained or ruined, and in my case, for the first time in my life, I felt that, for my safety, I should keep my political opinions to myself when out in public. It was beginning to feel different from the America I knew. The turning point was when Trump was nominated. Everyone went into political warfare mode and joined a tribe. The tension in the air became palpable. And dangerous.

Doug's Garage

Doug's garage was out on the county road, about a ten-minute walk from our place. Like a lot of rural Florida businesses, the auto repair shop he ran from a big steel building beside his house didn't require a sign or any other type of advertising other than word-of-mouth. If you were referred to him by a neighbor or friend, and he liked you, Doug would fix your car. Doug would handle most routine maintenance like brake jobs, oil changes, and tune-ups. If you showed up with something more complicated, he'd diagnose the problem and send you on your way to the auto parts store with a list of the things he'd need to get the job done. When he fixed your vehicle, he'd charge you about half of what a commercial garage would. Cash. Doug did not accept credit cards. But, there were times when friends of ours were out of work, and he fixed their cars, charging nothing more than a few dozen eggs from their hens, or a basket of tomatoes when the vines ripened. But if you crossed him, or became a pain-in-his-ass, he would never fix your car again. He'd tell you he was too busy, or refer you to a bigger shop in town with the excuse that he wasn't sure he knew how to diagnose and repair your vehicle's problem. After a few rejections, people would get the hint and stop asking. He had a high tolerance for most things, but lying to him, or being a general knucklehead would get you shit-canned from his good graces. Some people were devastated when Doug refused to service their vehicles. It was as if they were going through a divorce. He saved a lot of people much money and stress, including me.

In 2007, soon after marrying Jill and moving to Gilchrist County, I met Doug. But it wasn't because my car needed service. A friend of ours called Jimmy brought me over to Doug's garage for the initial interview. At the time, I was new to this little North Florida community, and the garage was something of a meeting place for the guys. On almost any morning there was a good chance that three or four men would be sitting around on metal folding chairs, shooting the shit, and watching Doug work on a car sitting up high on the lift. Doug was very social. He liked the company and invited the guys to bring their coffee cups and hang out with him. Doug's garage was the center of the local testosterone brain trust. I likened it to days gone by when men in their dusty coveralls would sit around a pot belly stove in the back room of the general store, solving the world's problems.

Among the married guys we had a running joke; we would tell our wives we were "going over to Doug's garage to watch him work." Some responded, "I should have married Doug." And maybe a few of the girls would have preferred him. He was tanned and handsome, a well-groomed guy with thick, curly black hair and a fit body. He had the core strength of a man who wrestles with metal and steel for a living. Doug had no reason to go to a gym. He was solid, and not just physically. Many people considered Doug the rock of our community. In every group there is a person who holds it all together. That was Doug. He was the catalyst. Politicians running for office would frequently visit to seek his approval. Doug was politically influential, and he prided himself on the weight that his opinion carried across the county. Every first Saturday of the month, the volunteer fire department located next to Doug's held a fund-raising pancake breakfast. During election season, candidates would attend the breakfast, glad-handing and smiling with the neighbors; then they'd slip around the gate to Doug's place and engage in the serious business of earning his endorsement.

Doug's influence stretched across many aspects of life, including the loosely organized citizen's militia. He was the de-facto leader of a small band of well-armed men whose infatuation with guns was, to me, troubling. They were prepping for the apocalypse. I'm sure some of these guys were still making payments on the stores of freeze-dried survivalist food and buckets of spoiled rice they bought during the run-up to Y2K. Now, they prepped for any impending catastrophe, real or imagined.

Living in Florida, where the weather can be violent and unpredictable, many families have a disaster plan. With hurricanes, floods, power outages, wildfires, and droughts, most of us have learned the value of emergency back-up generators and long-term supplies of food and water. I collected rainwater in 55-gallon drums, put up a few weeks worth of freeze-dried food, and had a pantry full of canned goods. I also kept a bountiful vegetable garden. If all else failed, I'd dig up my sweet potatoes, go down to the Santa Fe River and catch some fish, or trap and develop a taste for squirrel meat. It is a subject I never thought about growing up in Philadelphia, but on a ten-acre piece of land in the middle of the piney woods, I took pleasure in my self-sufficiency. Each week, as I tested our propane generator, the initial reluctant sputtering would transition to a reassuring gas-powered hum. Being ready for a few unplanned tropical storms with power outages was now part of my routine.

But the guys at Doug's garage, I soon learned, were preparing for scenarios well beyond what a vengeful Mother Nature could throw at them.

When I first moved to this part of Florida, the local men gave me a warm welcome. They knew my wife Jill, an acclaimed underwater explorer and filmmaker. She sometimes appeared on network television, and they had seen a lot of her work. Jill visited their kid's schools and gave them copies of her books and films at presentations. They were delighted that a woman living in their community was receiving international recognition.

I was recently out of the military in 2007 when I met this rag-tag citizen militia group. Having completed stints on active duty in the Navy SeaBees, and later, as a Staff Sergeant in the Army Reserve, I still maintained a hint of my military bearing. Many of these guys at Doug's were playing at being G.I. Joe, doing some half-assed infantry training in the woods. Not one of them had ever served in the armed forces. They bought ammo by the pallet load, chipping in on huge orders of .223 rifle rounds for their customized AR-15s. When they discovered I was a veteran, they enthusiastically invited me to join in their improvised field exercises. I had zero interest. I'd seen people like this all over the country, from Montana to Pennsylvania. I considered them "wanna-be" soldiers, and they were usually stupid and dangerous. But, because I had once worn expert marksman medals on my chest, they tried to draft me into their ranks. I attended some impromptu meetings at the garage, but never went on their tactical weekend warrior trips. Besides, I didn't have an A.R. I owned two rifles, an older .22 caliber Remington varmint gun, and a lever-action 30-30 Winchester cowboy rifle. Hardly enough firepower to take down the tyrannical "Powers That Be." The one thing I did acknowledge, was that American society was breaking down, a little at a time, and it would be nice to have some people around who were willing to ensure the community's safety until things could get sorted out. I became a reluctant, cynical, closet "Prepper."

"What caliber are you on?" Tim, one of the regulars at the garage and Doug's closest friend asked.

"Caliber?" I responded with a question.

"Yeah. We're all on .223. You should get your ass on .223 so when the shit-hits-the-fan you won't run out of ammo."

The whole shit-hits-the-fan scenario was something I've heard for a few decades. Every once in awhile, Americans seem to fear the end is nigh, and there is a run on gun sales and tin cans of beany-weiners.

"Well, what do you call the shit hitting the fan?" I asked Tim.

"The niggers. The niggers are coming," said Tim.

I wasn't accustomed to hearing the N-word so casually thrown around, and his response startled me a bit.

"You're shitting me, right?" I asked.

"No, Rob, the niggers from Gainesville and Jax are gonna come out here looking for food when the balloon goes up. Mark my words. Blacks don't prep. They suck on the government tit. When that tit runs dry, they are gonna' come all chimpin' out here 'cause they know we got food and water. Well, with God as my witness, they ain't gettin' me n' mine's."

Whoa! Even if Tim's nightmare was plausible, Gainesville was 35 miles away and Jacksonville about a hundred. There were a lot of deputies, police, and well-armed rednecks in-between. The probability that gangs of urban black men would somehow take to the countryside, looting and pillaging, was beyond ludicrous. Here was Tim and some of his compatriots using this twisted reasoning to justify their infatuation with the militia and guns. My facial expression must have betrayed my disbelief.

"Don't believe it, do you, Robert?" asked Doug.

"No, not really, it seems a bit dramatic," I said.

"What about the Feds?"

"What about them?"

"You know that if Obama gets elected, he's going to have the Feds come and get our A.R.s. Then they'll grab our hunting rifles and pistols."

Guns. These guys and their precious guns.

I said, "Doug if the Feds want your guns, your little A.R. pea-shooters aren't going to do shit against armored vehicles and helicopter gunships. Hell, they'll fire a tank round from a mile up the road that will blast right through your shop window, and you won't even know where it came from."

"No," he responded. "We're setting up roadblocks at the county line. Tractors and front-end loaders."

I gave up.

Geez. I was, at one time, a staff sergeant in an Army tank battalion. Even though I had real-life experience in M-1 Abrams tanks, these guys thought they knew better than me because they read some survivalist conspiracy forum on the Internet. They were a bunch of keyboard warriors, inspired by the likes of conspiracy media guru Alex Jones and his InfoWars website. And they were armed to the teeth and itching for an event that would allow them to "lock and load" and shoot someone. Preferably someone browner than themselves.

Over the years, I have remained good friends with Doug but made it clear that I thought the whole militia thing was dangerous and a waste of his time. I think some of my skepticism may have rubbed off. In time, he uncoupled himself from organized political groups. His enthusiasm for the promising grassroots Tea Party movement was soon tempered by the egotistical infighting he saw over local leadership and influence. His friend Tim accused me of being a covert communist. His prosecutorial evidence was my marriage to a "Libtard Socialist." I have a hunch that Ol' Tim sensed that I recognized his overcompensating toxic masculinity. I have called him out about it more than once.

The whole experience hanging out at Doug's garage opened my eyes to just how divided and fearful working-class Americans have become. And to be fair, they have a lot to be pissed off about. The policies of the globalist establishment caused many of their jobs to be shipped overseas, the result of a series of confusing trade agreements and treaties. The so-called New World Order didn't leave room for a blue-collared American working stiff. Cheap Chinese and Mexican labor helped propel corporate profits to the moon, but the American men and women who once built automobiles and refrigerators found themselves being asked to train their third world replacements and then go happily about trying to live on unemployment benefits or low-paying service jobs. It was the emasculation of the American working man, and it wasn't an accident. The institutions they once leaned on for guidance and support—churches, schools, banks, and trade unions, were broken or corrupted beyond repair. They suspected the mainstream media had become less interested in their plight and seemed to be a propaganda tool of the coastal elites. The stock market set record high after record high. And, while basking in unparalleled profits, Wall Street unmercifully fucked Main Street, draining every last drop of blood from small family businesses, replacing Mom and Pop shops with Walmarts and big box stores on the edge of town.

In 2008, Barack Obama, the first African-American man to be nominated by a major party, was overwhelmingly elected president. The preppers, survivalists, and racist gun-totin' militias of Redneck America went absolutely batshit. Jill and I enthusiastically voted for him.

God blessed America. Maybe for the last time.

A Libertarian Socialist

My working-class North Philadelphia upbringing, in a neighborhood of many first-generation Americans favored that, like my father, I'd be a registered Democrat. He leaned strongly to the progressive left-wing of the Democratic party, and, on occasion, admitted that he was a Socialist at heart. In post-war America, a man with a union job supported most families. The Democrats were the friend of the working man. Republicans, on the other hand, were the upper-class country club crowd. Regular people like us, who shopped with coupons to buy groceries, then used the brown bags they came in for school textbook covers, voted Democrat.

On our block was Johnny Hurley, a Democratic City committeeman, who could do miraculous things like getting traffic tickets fixed. He was a mid-level employee of the Philly public works department, but in his role as our neighborhood committeeman, he was nothing short of a prince. I don't think he ever paid for a beer down at McGuire's. When, in my early teens, I showed promise as a baseball player, Mr. Hurley recommended me to the manager of the Democratic Club's team. I was given a tryout and earned a spot on one of the most well-funded and talented youth baseball clubs in the city. Sitting on an air-conditioned bus traveling out of town to play rich kids on suburban fields, I felt like a major leaguer. In large block letters, the side of our bus announced "PHILADELPHIA DEMOCRATS." Although Benjamin Franklin was admittedly an Independent, the bus had a big picture of Ben wielding a Louisville Slugger on his shoulder.

When I turned eighteen, I quickly registered to vote. Not so much motivated by my civic duty, but more so that I could have that much-coveted voter's card in my wallet. You see, in Pennsylvania, the legal age to drink alcohol was twenty-one, but just across the bridge in New Jersey, it was eighteen. And like so many other young guys from Philly, I spent every summer weekend at the Jersey shore. (Long before it was a trendy MTV reality series, we were living it in real life). A voter I.D. was as good as gold in the Wildwood clubs, where you could buy three frosty draft beers for a dollar. The catch was they had to be ordered all at once, so the third one was usually pretty warm by the time you drank it. Yep, eighteen-year-olds slamming warm, cheap, rot-gut beers before they become too putrid to drink. What could go wrong?

I had to register for another important I.D. card after my eighteenth birthday– a Vietnam era Selective Service card. I came to believe it was only "selective" in that it never seemed to select rich white kids. The draft card was even more impressive than a voter I.D. The bouncers at Jersey bars would give us a nod when we flashed the draft cards. Also at some neighborhood bars in Philly, where the legal age was still 21, many bartenders figured that if you were old enough to get drafted and die for your country, you should be old enough to drink a few beers in their place.

Every time I think of that draft card I remember Billy Shay, the fastest runner in the neighborhood. He was tall and thin and moved like a gazelle. The high school track coach tried in vain to get Billy on the cross-country team. But Billy didn't like school, and he didn't like teams.

He just liked to run.

Once in awhile, Billy, who was about four years older than me, would play touch football on the street with us younger guys. There was only one set play; throw the ball as far as you could and Billy would run under it and catch it for a touchdown. He could have scored on every down. Billy had just landed a job with the Post Office and bought a brand new, dark blue Pontiac GTO with chromed Cragar mag wheels. He had long, dark, curly hair, and his shy smile captured every girl's eye each time he pulled up in that rumbling muscle car. Then, he was unexpectedly drafted into the Army a few months after he turned twenty. He went to boot camp and straight to Vietnam.

Billy's younger sister Susan was the most beautiful girl on our street. She had long blonde hair and the softest blue eyes I'd ever seen. When she smiled and said, "Hi Bobby" to me, I'd melt right into the pavement. With my pubescent mates, I'd sneak up the alley when she was on the back porch sunbathing in her bikini to get a glimpse of her. She dated another older guy named Steve, who was studying to be a physical education teacher. Steve had a draft deferment because he was in college. He was a good guy who played baseball for Temple University and helped take them to the College World Series. He, Billy and Susan were the best looking and most popular young people around.

One hot afternoon, I was in the corner store buying a Frank's cream soda when the lady behind the counter, Mrs. Angelo, dropped her black telephone to the floor and began wailing and praying in broken English-Italian. "What's the use…Perché Dio.Why? Why…?"

I tried to pay for the soda, but she kept saying, "Perché Dio," and other Italian words I couldn't understand. The tiny woman came out from behind the counter and grabbed my arm with a strong grip. It freaked me out. She squeezed harder and harder, saying in broken English, "Take them all...No!"...She looked me in the eye and said, "They take our Billy!... non piu...They can have no more!...No...non piu...!"

By the time I wrestled free of the distraught Mrs. Angelo and escaped back out to the street, the neighborhood was buzzing. Mothers and daughters were running to the Shay's house. Older women sat on the porch steps sobbing. The men from McGuire's were standing outside, holding half-empty glasses of beer and staring silently down at their shoes.

A taxi pulled up in front of the Shay's house with Billy's dad in the back seat. The driver got out and stood quietly next to his yellow cab. He didn't accept the fare when offered, he just took deep drags on his cigarette and squeezed Mr. Shay's shoulder as he walked by. Mr. Shay was in his brown work overalls from the plant where he was a foreman. A tall man, he towered over the women lining the sidewalk. He said nothing, made contact with no one, his black steel-toed boots trudged slowly up the steps and disappeared into the house.

A long gray Buick slowly turned the corner and parked on the sidewalk across from the house. Out stepped Father Graham, from Saint Helen's. The Shay's went to public school, and I didn't know they were Catholic. The priest made the sign of the cross as he walked past the older women. They blessed themselves, and some clutched rosaries.

My friends Dan and Jerry Boyle ran up to me.

"Billy Shay got killed!" Jerry blurted out.

"Holy shit!" I said.

"They said he knifed the 'Cong that shot him!" Added Dan.

Then I saw my father.

He walked over to the Boyle brothers and me. It was two in the afternoon on a weekday and the only other time my dad came home early from work was after the assassination of John Kennedy. My father, a robust and redheaded carpenter, reached over and put one big arm around my neck and wrapped the two Boyle boys in the other.

"Let's go, lads, show's over. Your mothers will be wanting you near today."

Soon after Billy's funeral, Susan and Steve broke up and I never saw her blue eyes smiling again.

The war in Vietnam raged on.

A few years later, when I turned eighteen and received my draft card, all the sadness about Billy came back to me. The Nixon White House had suspended the draft, as the war was winding down. No more young men would be conscripted to die in the jungle. I was required to register but luckily, would not have to go.

Ironically, as much as I avoided military service in my teens, a few years and a lot of mileage later, I enlisted in the Navy. Because we were not actively engaged in a fighting war, I felt that the service was a safe way to get my 25-year-old shit together, figure out what I wanted to do with my life, and land back on my feet when I finished my enlistment.

After nine years on active Navy duty, followed by a stint in the Army Reserves, my political viewpoint slowly began to change. There were a lot of conservative influences on me from my senior officers and career enlisted friends. I was listing to the right. It felt important to me, to be accepted by my peers and I was yielding to the pressure to get in line with the conservative dogma. By the early nineties, Bill Clinton was president and I was sipping the

Kool-Aid served up by Newt Gingrich, Pat Buchanan and other leaders of the newly empowered right-wing. Even though a part of me knew I was betraying my late father's memory, I changed my voter registration to Republican. I justified my actions by telling myself the world was transforming quickly, and Dad would understand. I was very unsettled and in transition. I had spent a long time in the military, and I had no idea how to fit in with civilian society. I did not know what I believed or where I stood, so I capitulated to the dominant right-wing culture in which I was immersed.

In 1995, a Navy friend helped me land a spot as the co-host of a local talk radio call-in show. My new conservative public profile was rising considerably, and I enjoyed the attention lavished on me by the local GOP leadership. Like almost every caller-driven program, the subject was politics, politics, and more politics. The populist radio movement was in full swing with shows like Chuck Harder's "For the People," featuring guests like independent presidential candidate Ross Perot. On the far right was Watergate conspirator G. Gordon Liddy's radio show, where his alfa-male viewpoints were burning up the airwaves. A fledgling Alex Jones' Infowars capitalized on the public's shock over the Waco and Ruby Ridge incidents and pushed suspicion of Bill Clinton's globalist agenda. Conservative radio voices were the loudest and most likely to be syndicated and I harbored secret ambitions to be the next Rush Limbaugh. Our show's listening area was limited to the Florida Panhandle and southern Alabama, and we enjoyed decent ratings and regional success. Many opportunities presented themselves simply because I had access to a microphone and transmitter tower five afternoons a week.

My head swelled when I was asked to sit on the County Republican Executive Committee. Remembering Committeeman Johnny Hurley from Philly, and how he was held in such high regard by the neighborhood, I jumped at the chance to be officially involved in politics. Here I was, being courted by some of the most influential people in a large Florida county to come and sit at the big table. It all went to my head, and I became an instant young Republican asshole. I dressed differently, talked differently, and even married a young, conservative Christian woman. I took up golfing! Wearing those frat boy golf shirts and hobnobbing with the movers and shakers at the club, I betrayed everything my father instilled in me about the working-class ideal. I thought I was a big shot. I hopped on the right-wing bandwagon because it was a formidable force in the place I lived and worked. I even joined my wife's conservative church. Our radio show became the North Florida conduit for ultra-conservative candidate Pat Buchanan's presidential bid. We were thrilled when he called in and spoke to us on the show. I volunteered to help run his local campaign office. When we were low on funds for Buchanan lawn signs and advertising, two mysterious guys from the little town of Milton showed up with a couple of checks to cover the costs. We reported the donation correctly, and it was all clean and legal. About a month later I found out they were with the Florida Knights of the Ku Klux Klan. Deep down, I knew this was all a charade on my part, and accepting donations from klansmen may have been an all-time low for me. But, at the time, I was highly ambitious and trying to reinvent myself in this new town, and conservatism opened doors and smoothed the path. I played along.

One of the sponsors of our radio show, a wealthy real estate investor, invited me to an unusual political meeting. He didn't elaborate; he just told me that most of the serious conservative constitutional types would be attending. Like Pat Buchanan, I often described myself as a "Constitutionalist," rather than "Conservative." It gave me cover for some pretty biased opinions and made me feel somewhat more comfortable in this new skin I was trying on. I felt like I was serving something nobler, some cause superior to party politics. After all, as a serviceman, I took an oath to defend the Constitution against all enemies, foreign and domestic. At this point, I was almost brainwashed that the Liberal Democrats under the Clintons were the domestic enemy. Sound familiar?

When I walked into the special meeting, my antennae were on high alert. I was a bit nervous. I realized it was some type of secret society. About twenty men, all white, and dressed in business casual attire sat around a big table in the conference room of the local library branch. The uniform of the day was button-collared shirts and Dockers khakis. On a side table were carefully placed stacks of brochures and magazines. Most prominent were red, white and blue flyers, bumper stickers and pamphlets urging the U.S. to get out of the United Nations. I'd seen billboards extolling this same cause on the Interstate highway north of town. A glossy, high-quality magazine called "The New American" was placed on the seat of each chair, a bit of free conservative swag. I was at my first John Birch Society meeting!

I heard that the Birchers were as far to the right as one could legally get in America. Their stated mission to keep

Congress accountable, and educating the public about the Constitution made a lot of sense, but even at this first meeting I smelled a not-so-thinly-veiled streak of racism among the die-hard Birchers in the room. There were numerous expose's and articles written in the 70s' calling the Society radical racists and closed-minded bigots. After all, they did oppose civil rights legislation and the Equal Rights Amendment. But, that aside, what appealed to me as I sat in the meeting was a sense that these men knew more than I did. They had uncovered some secret agenda of the New World Order to take over America and turn us into a third-world level slave camp. They opposed the Federal Reserve, international banking, and trade cartels. The John Birch Society advocated for the Second Amendment and espoused state's rights. And, the JBS prided itself as one of the last bulwarks against a communist takeover of the United States. They saw creeping socialism as the first step in a well-orchestrated plan to bring America down. More than anything else, I wanted to have the secret knowledge. I was very impressionable at this point in my political development and the JBS appealed to me as the only organization that was serious about preserving our American values and way of life. We even pledged allegiance to the flag before the meeting, and ended it with an off-key rendition of "God Bless America." Who wouldn't want a piece of that sexy patriotic action, eh?

The elder Birch statesmen sent me off with an armload of books and reading material. The Creature from Jekyll Island, The Establishment's Man, and En Route to Global Occupation, were my initial JBS primer assignments. I read them voraciously. Each chapter exposed the hidden agenda of the Left to move America closer to communism, where women, gays and brown minorities would undermine all that White European Americans had built over two hundred-plus years. Merging into a socialist collective, along with Europe, the United Nations would send blue-helmeted Dutch and Belgian troops to confiscate our guns and march all the true patriots to concentration camps at abandoned U.S. military bases and train yards throughout the country. With the blessing of the Federal Reserve Bank, the U.S. dollar would be absorbed into some North American "Amero" currency at a fraction of its current value. (Birchers were big on accumulating physical gold.) I read every page of every issue of the New American magazine that I could get my hands on. In short order I became convinced that I was one of them, a true patriot, keeper of the Republic, one of the last brave men left to expose the New World Order and "take America back!" (This seems to be an eternal rallying cry of the right. My question today is: Take America back from whom?) The John Birch Society was, is, and will always be rooted in racism and fear of progressive change.

My Bircher mentor, a real estate broker named Harry, was the local chapter president. One day we were driving over to the studio to do some voiceover work. Harry had to take care of some landlord business on the way. We pulled into a gravel driveway leading to a sad-looking double-wide trailer. There was a beat-up pick up truck and a bunch of children's toys strewn in the front yard. A red curtain blew in and out of a broken storm window. It was a tough living situation. Hearing Harry's diesel Mercedes pull up, the young man, shirtless in only gym shorts and flip flops, popped out of the trailer and met Harry as he got out of the car.

"Where's my rent money, Junior?" Harry yelled.

"It's comin' Mr. Harry. My wife ain't got paid from the hospital yet and..."

Bam! Harry grabbed Junior by the waistband and slammed him onto the steaming hot hood of the car. Holding the sweaty, young shirtless man in a headlock, Harry reached behind his back, unholstered a Glock and pressed the metal barrel into Junior's temple.

"Don't you fuck with me, Junior!"

"No Mr. Harry, no sir!"

Junior twisted his way loose from Harry's grip and ran behind the trailer and into the woods.

Harry picked up the notebook and pen that fell from his shirt pocket and slid the gun back into its hidden holster; he eased back into the car.

"That'll be one less useless nigger in the world if he doesn't have the rent money come the end of the week," he said.

I was stunned. Here we were, out on a desolate Florida limestone road, miles from the next big town, and all I wanted to do was get out of the car and, like the poor soul Junior, run through the woods away from this maniac. But I had to play it cool.

"Holy shit, Harry!" I said. "What was that about?"

"That my friend was about how niggers need to be put down when they fuck with white men. They are blue-gummed savages and, if they think they can get over on me, I'll put the fear of God into them before they know which way is up."

"I don't know! God damn Harry, you could have killed that guy." I said.

"That guy gets killed, who cares? Just one less porch monkey sucking on the welfare tit and breathing white man's air. Fuck him...he's a parasite. Let him get a real job and a better place if he doesn't want to pay me rent. Next time I'll put a round in his black ass!"

So, this was Harry Watkins, the stalwart leader of the local chapter of the John Birch Society. I did the radio spot with him, and as soon as we got back home, I got out of his car and never spoke with him or went to a JBS meeting again. My eyes were opening. I was guilty of betraying my roots. My conservative life suddenly felt like a farce. Over the next few months I ended my daily radio talk show and tried to turn it into a weekly magazine-style human interest program. It turns out, not many humans were that interesting, or at least interested in the subjects I presented, and, rather unceremoniously, it folded. My GOP co-host focussed his efforts on a cable-access political T.V. broadcast, and he did alright with it for a few years. That is, until he was indicted for helping some Florida State legislators move dark money around. I got out of media for many years until I began writing and producing documentary films and podcasts. None of which have anything to do with politics.

This conservative phase of mine lasted as long as the marriage to my fundamentalist Christian wife. We met at Alcoholics Anonymous, and our relationship only thrived in our mutual recovery. As I was transitioning from Liberal Progressive to Conservative Libertarian and back again, I also got sober. My sobriety allowed me to reinvent myself in ways I could never have imagined - and I tried on a few distorted versions of myself until I came back to the realization of who I am: a working-class Progressive Democrat. My little foray into GOP politics never felt quite honest. My father's spirit was always hovering around my shoulders, smacking me upside the head, attempting to get through to me, and navigate a path back to my truth. I was trying to be someone else's idea of what a man my age, in my circumstances should be. I slowly eased away from political activism and my marriage. It had never been a great choice for either of us. We both landed on our feet, and when I last checked, she was still a Republican Christian living out in the Rockies waiting for Jesus to come down from the clouds and pass judgment on all of us Democrat heathens. I squint and scan the audience when Trump holds his "I Love Me" rallies in western U.S. arenas. I keep waiting to see my ex show up holding a "Women for Trump" sign behind the podium. So far, no sign of her, but thousands of her clones keep attending to support this misogynistic man-boy. I will never understand how women can be personally or politically attracted to this admitted sexual predator. It will remain one of the great mysteries of our time.

I changed my voter party registration back to Democratic and recalculated my preferences in women back to the liberal, educated, just-this-side-of hippie artistic types that I always found attractive.

Over the last decade or so, I've voted for and supported progressive candidates of the Democratic or Green parties. Yes, I admit it, I voted for Ralph Nader and was one of the Florida voters responsible for the great Bush-Gore hanging chad fiasco. Maybe if some of us that voted for dear old Ralph had given Al Gore a nod, history would be written much differently today. I can't wait for affordable time machines, because this is something we should all do - travel back and vote overwhelmingly for Gore. Wishful thinking.

Today, I label myself a Democratic Socialist with Libertarian tendencies. By this, I mean that I subscribe to a "live and let live" philosophy, but, I admit that some people need a hand up. Some people need enhanced opportunities and the safety net that only a caring community can provide. I may be an enigma, but I think that the two philosophies, Libertarianism and Socialism are not mutually exclusive. When practical, some independent, skilled, well-off people can be as free as possible and have very little voluntary involvement with the government—Libertarian. But, not everyone is wired this way. Some people, for reasons and circumstances beyond their control, need government assistance as they pursue health and happiness—Socialist. As a partially-disabled American Veteran, I benefit from the healthcare and small stipend I receive from the Veteran's Administration—Socialist. As an independent, self-employed person, I enjoy the freedoms of choice and security granted by the Constitution—Libertarian. Therefore, I am a Libertarian Socialist. There is no such thing as the Libertarian Socialist party in America, so, I identify with my Democratic friends.

As I prepare to become a Canadian Permanent Resident, and eventually a citizen, it is almost inevitable that I continue to compare and contrast the U.S. political parties to their Canadian equivalents. I'd have to classify the U.S. Republicans as the closest party to the Conservative Party of Canada. In fact, upon closer inspection, the Canadian Conservatives are more in line with the American centrist, or moderate ideology. Stephen Harper was the long-time

Conservative Canadian Prime Minister, and well-known to many Americans. Andrew Sheer is the current Conservative leader. Moving from right to left, the Liberal Party of Canada is pretty darn close to the American Democratic Party. The Liberals currently hold power in Canada, and Prime Minister Justin Trudeau is one of Trump's chief nemesis'.

If the socialist wing of the American Democratic Party teamed up with the Greens, the Canadian equivalent would be the New Democratic Party. The charismatic Sikh-Canadian, Jagmeet Singh, leads the "NDP." Independence-minded French speakers are represented by the Bloc Quebecois and Mario Beaulieu. There is not an American party similar to the Bloc Quebecois, as their power is born from ideas of separating French Canada from the rest of the country. Canada has dozens of officially recognized parties including the environmentally-conscious Green Party (similar to their U.S. cousins) and a handful of regional and provincial parties. There is even a Marijuana Party of Canada, and now that recreational cannabis is entirely legal, they may not need any more recruits.

One of the things that Americans (including me) have a hard time getting our heads around is the relationship between Canada and Great Britain. Or England. Or the

United Kingdom. Or the British Commonwealth... whatever it is called. Elizabeth II is officially the Queen of Canada. Huh? Yes, the Queen we all know and love is the Canadian Head of State. Representing the Queen in Ottawa, is a figurehead without real power, the Canadian Governor General. Currently, the Governor General is Julie Payette, the former astronaut. That's kind of cool. I met the previous Governor General David Johnston a few times as Jill received recognitions and awards from her government. (Well, he won't remember me, but we had a handshake, a few words, and a selfie. That counts, right?)

Canada is (according to Wikipedia) a "Westminster style federal parliamentary democracy within a constitutional monarchy." So, unlike the United States, which is, for the most part, a two-party system, Canada has a multi-party Parliament. Within that body, whichever party holds the most seats gets to form a government and select a Prime Minister, much like the British. Canadians don't vote directly for their federal leader, but instead vote for their local Member of Parliament or M.P.

The Liberal Party currently has more members of Parliament, followed by the Conservatives and then the NDP and Bloc Quebecois. There is a House of Commons, similar to the United States House of Representatives and

Canada has an appointed, not elected, Senate, similar to (you guessed it) the United States Senate. The Prime Minister also appoints various ministers, just as the U.S. president selects their Cabinet.

Canada is a relatively young country. My wife, Jill (because she was born before 1982), came into this world as a Canadian subject of Queen Elizabeth II. Jill's family traces their roots back to the early 1700s, settling in the English Loyalist towns of southern Ontario. She claims it was her mother's family that helped burn down the White House during the War of 1812. It was the Canada Act in 1982 that established complete sovereignty as an independent country, although the Queen retained her role as monarch of Canada. (That's the part I don't understand.) Most Canadians agree that Confederation occurred on July 1st, 1867, when Canada established a Constitution. Today, "Canada Day" is a significant federal holiday and celebration, much like the July 4th Independence Day in the U.S.

Something for my American friends to ponder: according to a recent study by The Economist, Canada is considered the most stable democracy in the Americas, and the 3rd most democratic country in the entire world. In the same study, the United States ranked 18th. Canada, with a population of only 37 million people, has the 10th largest economy, measured by GDP, in the world. The much more populous United States is firmly number one, followed by China and Japan.

All of this is well and good; however, what makes Canada so attractive to me is its emphasis on social welfare, economic freedom and multiculturalism. Simply put, Canadians take care of each other. The Canadian Charter of Rights and Responsibilities not only spells out the rights that each Canadian enjoys, but also the civic responsibilities those rights entail. The United States also has a Bill of Rights baked into its founding documents, but the citizenry lacks a sense of responsibility.

My wife explained to me once that as a child, she was taught that Canada is a mosaic of cultures. Unlike Trump's America, which claims to be a melting pot, but is, in reality, boiling over with animus towards migrants, Canada embraces immigrants, encouraging them to maintain their customs and languages. A few years ago, I was riding the subway in Toronto. Across from me sat two Muslim women in traditional hijabs, a Black guy wearing a Maple Leafs hockey sweater, and a Buddhist monk dressed in a saffron robe. They were all engaged in a heavily-accented

English language conversation about the unseasonably hot weather.

In a nutshell, this is Canada.

Another experience I'd like to share: We were in a diner in the Francophone Ontario town of Sturgeon Falls. (I never knew there were French speakers outside of Quebec.) A rather large, multigenerational, multiracial family occupied a big round table at the center of the restaurant. The family patriarch, a white guy who was probably in his seventies, loudly exclaimed to the younger people around him, "I don't know what to call some of your kids. They are mixed oriental, black and white. Are they White, Chinese, or Negro?" To which his daughter replied, "No daddy, they are Canadian. Just call them what they are, your Canadian grandchildren."

This, my dear American friends, is Canada.

My theory is that Canadian winters are so harsh, so inherently dangerous, that people must learn to get along with one another. You never know when your Chinese/Syrian/Sikh neighbor is going to buy a new snowblower and become the most popular person on the street, and, hopefully, your new best friend.

We Can't Stay Here

I proudly voted for Barack Obama. Twice. That is, in two separate elections, not twice fraudulently in each election as the right-wing conspiracy theorists would have you believe. Never has a candidate resonated with my core beliefs as much as Mr. Obama did. America hadn't seen this sense of optimism and hope since the days of John F. Kennedy. I was only six years old when an assassin's bullet took JFK, but it is easy to see the correlation between what Kennedy's election meant to the Irish-American communities of the sixties, and Obama's to the African-American communities of 2008. Although my family ancestry goes back to Scotland, we lived in an Irish neighborhood, were taught by nuns at Irish-Catholic schools, and identified with the Irish. If your family had a "Mc" or an "O" preceding its last name, everyone just assumed they were from Ireland. My paternal great-grandfather came to America from Dumfries and Galloway in southwest Scotland, by way of Armagh in today's Northern Ireland – A Roman Catholic family passing through Protestant British territory. My grandmother was born in Yorkshire, in England. Philadelphia became their place to pursue the American dream. I am the first American-born male member of my family to attend college and have a real shot at fulfilling that American ideal. Except, I now choose to live in Canada.

During the 2008 presidential primary season, Mr. Obama spoke a language I understood. I felt comfortable with his message of hope and change. He was a big city guy like me. He seemed sincere, articulate, and addressed the issues that are important to working people. His health care plans were compelling and necessary. I already had excellent health care coverage from the V.A., but I knew many Americans who had little to no help when it came to their medical expenses. (I still think that we could provide universal healthcare if we just adopted the Veteran's Administration medical template and extended it to everyone.) In 2008 I was working as an independent nurse contractor at Florida prisons. As a prison nurse, I interacted with inmates, security staff, and administration every day. It baffled me that the prisoners had better access to medical resources than the guards who minded them. The guards, or more accurately, "Correctional Officers," were underpaid, over-worked and had their medical and retirement benefits cut back or outright slashed as the state made substantial budget cuts and moved to a privatized for-profit prison model.

Although they were State of Florida employees, the prison workers medical insurance was expensive, with high co-pays and gaps in coverage. But, considering the scarce alternatives in rural areas, working outside the prison for less pay and zero benefits, many of the guards and staff soldiered on, coming to work every day in a dangerous, understaffed environment because they had to provide for their families. I asked many of them if they would leave their prison jobs if something else were available to them, some position with decent pay and a good benefits package. Almost every single one expressed that they hated their current jobs and would leave in a heartbeat if given a chance. A State Prison is not the healthiest environment to go to every day. They are already overcrowded, understaffed in the security and medical departments, and very stressful, dangerous workplaces. Add to that mix, dissatisfaction with pay and benefits, and you have a culture ripe for cheating, abuse, and corruption. Many corrections personnel were making extra money by smuggling contraband into the prisons on their work shifts. Everything from drugs to cell phones was available via the guards if an inmate had the cash. And, as the guards became more corrupted and compromised, they were blackmailed to the point of being under the thumb of highly organized and violent gangs. And all of this violence and corruption could have been avoided if the state paid the prison employees a decent middle-class wage along with medical coverage and a basic retirement package. You know, like it used to be when we had powerful trade unions and true leadership at the state and federal level.

Besides the correctional officers, I knew of several other men my age who thought they were set for life because of their excellent jobs. I watched them get down-sized or replaced as the economy flat-lined during the real estate crash. A friend from Doug's garage suddenly found himself laid off, upside down on his second mortgage, and running out of medical coverage for his chronically sick wife. He had to sell his Harley at a loss to cover a few months of her prescription medications. This was a guy with graduate school education and a licensed profession. The company he worked at for eight years replaced him with a younger man willing to work for a fraction of the salary. He lost all the unemployment appeals, as Florida is a "right to work" state. This term can be confusing because Florida is a "right to be fired for any reason whatsoever" state. I was never a big fan of this guy, but watching him suffer and barely scrape by was not pretty. Eventually, he took an under-the-table cash job as he tried to get something more permanent. Well, something more permanent never came, and he is now working for almost minimum wage at a retail store in town. He was never someone you'd call happy, but now he's downright miserable and mean. He and his poor, sick wife are aging rapidly, and things don't look too promising for either of them. Watching this was a great eye-opener for me. I swore I'd never be in that position, where an employer could fire me or downsize me into poverty.

I decided to take a big gamble and quit nursing to work for my wife's small media production company. One of the most significant factors allowing me to change careers in my fifties was that I had medical coverage through the V.A., and it followed me anywhere I went (even to Canada). I wished everyone could be free to choose where they worked and went to school, or simply decide to pursue a creative endeavor, knowing that they would have medical insurance. But, not in the U.S. of A. Somewhere along the line, American society chose to attach healthcare coverage to a person's employment, so every day millions of people trudge their sick, broken bodies to a job they hate, just because they need their utterly inadequate healthcare insurance.

God forbid these miserable, unhealthy people become seriously ill, or have a life-threatening accident. Many of them, even though they thought they had insurance, wind up bankrupted by all the costs that the insurance companies do not pay. The majority of American personal bankruptcies are directly related to medical expenses that people thought were covered by their insurance.

So, beyond his eloquence, intelligence and policies close to my heart, the remote chance that most Americans would be able to get affordable, comprehensive health care coverage was enough for me to vote for Barack Obama. In 2008, the first African-American man to be nominated by a major party was overwhelmingly elected president. On the day he was inaugurated in January of 2009, I was sitting in the lobby of the V.A. Medical Center at Lake City, Florida. I was so moved by what I experienced, that I wrote this essay:

January 20, 2009. It is 12:15 p.m.

His long, angular brown face is crowned with a neatly groomed shock of closely cropped white hair. Pinned near the collar of his yellow windbreaker is the eagle device of a full bird colonel. Over his heart is an American flag pin and a miniature silver star medal.

The sofa on which he sits is too low, and his lanky legs are splayed in front of him. Cream-colored argyle socks complement his spit-shined soft brown oxfords.

In the corner of this, the lobby of the Lake City V.A. Medical Center sits a huge flat-screened television. Gathered around are dozens of people, some staff, some patients, all transfixed by the crisp image beaming around the world from the U.S. Capitol steps.

It is solemn and quiet in this space. The sound of the automatic door sliding open and closed is the only external distraction. Whishing, whirring. Whishing, whirring. All eyes remain on the T.V.

On the screen is a   tall, handsome, young African-American man, his right hand raised. His left is resting on Abraham Lincoln's Bible.

He recites the oath of office as President of the United States.

The brown-faced man on the sofa buries his face in his hands and sobs. He reaches over to me, sitting in the stuffed institutional armchair to his right, takes my hand and cups it is both of his. His skin feels like warm, soft, boney leather. He squeezes my hand and leans closer.

"Eighty-one years," he says in a hoarse whisper. "Eighty-one years I fought for this..."

I squeeze his hands firmly, look him straight in the eye, and we sit there counting the heartbeats of the moment. Two veterans from different wars,   different worlds, breathing the same air, sharing and sobbing.

January 20, 2009. America has a chance to become a better country today.

When Obama was elected, the white supremacists and Alt-Right militias of America went batshit. Jill and I voted for him. My friend from Doug's garage, the one who lost his job, and almost lost his home and wife, did not.

He was among the many white male friends and acquaintances that wanted to dump me when I told them I voted for Barack. They can kiss my ass. In spite of their narrow-minded racism, America set a course to be a better country on January 20, 2009. Ask the Colonel, a brave man who fought in two wars and patiently waited eighty-one hard years to see the nearly impossible become a reality.

Barack Obama's hand laid across Abraham Lincoln's bible - that's the America in which I want to believe. But Donald Trump, enabled by the Republican Party, is doing everything he can to undo any progress made during the

Obama years. They are gutting the Affordable Care Act. They are giving tax breaks to the rich while dismantling policies and programs that help the poor and working class. With Trump's willful ignorance of foreign affairs, international trade and treaties, he is chasing away American jobs at Harley-Davidson, General Motors, Ford, and dozens of medium and small manufacturers from coast to coast. Donald Trump, his family, and their business partners are using his presidency to enrich themselves, with little regard for what is right for the country as a whole.

During the first year of the Trump administration, I hoped that the gravity of the office, and the responsibilities, traditions and cultural norms of the presidency would sink in, and he'd rise to a higher calling. Nope. Instead, Trump's disregard for the sanctity and service required by the Oval Office may have damaged the presidency forever.

I never believed America was the best place on earth. I saw her faults, her smudged makeup through her tears, her anger, and her character defects in all their high definition glory. But, I always thought America was working to be the best she could be. After eight years of Obama's idealism, the election of Donald Trump shattered that illusion for me.

America: What the fuck were you thinking? How the American people could select this mean-spirited sociopathic con-man to be our leader says a whole lot more about where America's collective soul is than it does about Trump. What is even more troubling is the number of people who continue to support him, whether in the halls of Congress or from the cheap seats at his Third Reich-style rallies.

I have reached the point where I sincerely fear for America's future. I have abandoned all the optimism and hope I recently evoked, generated in part by two terms of Barack Obama. My positivity has been eroded by the tangible threat to democracy Donald Trump and his followers personify.

"Jill, my love," I recently said when we still lived in Florida, "This is what it must have felt like in Germany during the 1930s' idly standing by as Hitler rose to power."

"We can't stay here, and idly stand by," she replied.

From that moment, we began to plan our departure from Donald Trump's America.

Guns

About the time we met, Jill and I were both recovering from complicated divorces. Urged by friends and family, we coincidentally decided to place personal ads on the same Internet dating site. Each time I checked it, Jill's profile kept coming up as a 100% match. I stared at her picture and profile for a long time, reading every word, studying the construction of her sentences, trying to get some insight into who this perfectly matched person was. For days I was trying to muster the courage to contact her. I wrote, edited, deleted, and re-wrote a dozen messages before finally crafting the one I wanted to send. I was approaching fifty-years-old, and she appeared a bit younger. I liked what I saw on her profile, and hoped to get her attention. I could tell from the few hints she placed on the site that she was an accomplished person. I gathered the courage to hit the send button and held my breath.

For the next few days, I obsessively checked my messages, hoping that she had responded. Nope. Nothing. After a week, I began to lose hope. Oh well. Maybe something about me didn't click with her. I was open and honest in my original message and told her I was sober and in recovery for many years. Shit! I shouldn't have been so forthright. I didn't have to over-share in my very first message. Shit! Shit! Shit!

I resigned myself to staying single. I had dated some nice women, but no one attracted my long-term interest. In this regard, I sometimes felt like an insanity magnet. Many of the women I met carried baggage from failed relationships, addictions or sadly, they were abused beyond my ability to help with repairs. I asked myself why I kept attracting broken people and wondered if subconsciously I was seeking someone who needed fixing. Some women turned out to be a little more broken than others, and I hit the exit pretty quickly with them. I didn't want a middle-aged relationship renovation project. I enjoyed female company, so I spent some casual time with a few of them, going for coffee or lunch. But the profile of the 100-percent match woman still intrigued me. Maybe it was just my fantasy, the idea that someone who was a perfect match was out there looking for me too. Damn you Internet! Why did you dangle that perfect profile in front of me? Then, in my sharply-honed conspiracy theorist mind, I deduced that Ms.100% match was just a bot— a troll placed by the dating service to get me to upgrade and pay for a membership each month. She didn't exist. I was sure of it. My obsession with Ms.100% faded into casual interest, and I stopped checking the messages. I reluctantly moved on.

Then, about two weeks later, it happened! I got a response! She's real!

I read and re-read her message. The basic gist of it was, "Hey, sorry I haven't responded, I've been busy and without an Internet connection. I'm working on a documentary film in the field. I want to communicate some more, but please be patient until I get out of this swamp and can talk to you."

Oh, my God! Patience was not my strong suit, but I considered this a great sign. I would wait for her. But, in the meantime, I had to craft the perfect reply to her response. So, back to the messaging platform of the dating site. Again, I must have said something that piqued her interest, because I received a reply that very night. She must still have access to wifi, somewhere. We arranged, over the next few messages to move our correspondence over to our email, and stop using the hard to navigate and clunky messaging on Yahoo! Dating. Cool. We were stepping it up a notch.

When we first corresponded via email, Jill was finishing production work for a four-part PBS series called "Water's Journey." She was on location in the Florida Everglades, literally up to her ass in alligators. (She is unlike any other woman I have ever met.) When we finally had our first "real" date, I was instantly mesmerized and quite smitten by this remarkable woman. I know special when I see it, and Jill is nothing, if not an exceptional human being. Our first date started with a stroll at a beautiful spring at a Florida State Park and went well into the night sitting on an outside patio at a local restaurant. As we walked the trails at the spring and later sat talking at the diner, I knew she was the one. The entire world melted away, and it was just Jill and me in a universe all our own. I know that "love at first sight" is an overused and sometimes trivial phrase, but I was experiencing it. I knew from that first evening she was the person I wanted to spend the rest of this, and hopefully many other lifetimes with. I had a troubling history of sabotaging most things that were good for me, so my mantra in the early days of our relationship was, "Just don't fuck it up."

When we first began dating, Jill had just finished building a custom house on ten forested acres in north Florida. The site she chose is very close to one of the scuba diving capitals of the world, the underwater caves at Ginnie Springs. Cave divers are the elite of the technical diving scene, and Jill is among the top practitioners. Considered one of the most dangerous activities in the world, many people have become familiar with cave divers through the recent dramatic rescue of the young Thai soccer team from inside a flooded cave. The divers who led that rescue effort are Jill's friends, dive buddies, and professional colleagues. During the Thai cave event, she was on an Arctic expedition helping to shoot a documentary film for the popular Canadian series, "The Nature of Things." While the rescue unfolded, Jill was called on by international news organizations for her expertise, to comment on and help explain the intricacies of cave diving and cave rescues. Jill herself has been a part of several cave rescue attempts and body recoveries. She has, unfortunately, lost some good friends and colleagues over a few decades of cutting edge exploration and diving. Today, Jill is celebrated as one of the top underwater photographers, explorers and adventure writers on the planet.

As a bonus, Jill shared with me her beautiful homeland. I had been to Canada a few times in the past, usually driving up from the Midwest to make deliveries when, after leaving the Navy, I briefly worked for a trucking company.

I got to spend a little bit of time between freight runs in some small Ontario towns. I'd usually park my big truck at the local hockey arena and set out to explore the area on the mountain bike I kept strapped behind the cab. Small, main street Ontario towns reminded me of America in the sixties and seventies. Mom and Pop shops, pubs, cafes, diners, hardware stores. All the things Walmart and Dollar Stores have chased from towns in Middle America. In the bigger Canadian cities like Toronto and Calgary, big box stores like Lowes, Home Depot and Best Buy were making inroads, but just outside the green belt that surrounds most Canadian cities, the main street is very much alive and well. I liked being in Ontario. It felt safe and comfortable. It was clean. People were wide awake and engaged with one another. I never imagined I'd be back later living here.

Early in our relationship, Jill and I traveled to Toronto, so I could meet her parents and the rest of her family. We drove up through the December snow for a Christmas get together. As we approached the New York/Canada border crossing at Buffalo, I suddenly remembered that I had a small pistol in my backpack, buried deep in the back of our van! If there is one significant difference between Canadian and American culture, it is the attitude toward guns. In Canada, it is almost impossible for an average person to carry a handgun. The licensing, permits, training, and security screenings are so vigorous that only very few people can legally possess a firearm. There must be an overwhelming reason in Canada to grant permission for an individual to carry a handgun. There are gun clubs, shooting ranges, and sportsmen groups who own and regularly shoot guns. However, unlike in the States, the firearms must be stored securely at the range or club, and not stuck into a waistband or holster to bring home. There is zero tolerance towards guns at the border crossings. If an American, like me, who is licensed, trained and experienced with firearms in my home state, is caught trying to enter Canada with a gun in a backpack, there will be hell to pay. It is almost certain to result in a criminal charge and jail time, along with a lifetime ban from the country. If the Canadian Border officers found my little . 380 Ruger stashed down next to my fresh underwear in my pack, it would instantly and negatively change my life.

Jill was driving as we approached the border. About a mile out I saw the sign listing the contraband items not permitted into Canada - particularly the handgun in the red circle with the diagonal slash through it, the international symbol for, "No firearms permitted."

"Holy shit, honey, I just remembered I have a gun in my pack!" I said.

Jill immediately pulled the van over to the shoulder.

"What? Are you kidding me?" she said.

"Nope, I forgot to pull it out before we left."

"Oh, Robert, that's a problem. We have to turn around."

So, she did a quick u-turn onto a highway ramp about a kilometer from the border crossing and began heading back into New York. We hadn't yet arrived at the border station, so luckily we could get off the road and regroup.

I could see that Jill was nervous and upset. I'd never seen her like this before.

"Robert, you can't make mistakes like this! If you get caught you'll never be able to get into Canada, and they might charge me because I'm driving. This is serious."

"Okay honey," I said, trying to lower the tension level. "We can just go back into Buffalo and take care of it."

I felt like an idiot. Jill wasn't very thrilled that I owned guns in the first place. When we decided to live together, it took a lot of effort to convince her that I was a responsible, safe, gun owner and eventually she accepted that I usually carried a handgun with me out in the world. The American world that is. But, in Canada, it was a different story.

When I told my buddies from Doug's garage that I was heading up to Canada for the holidays, more than one of them said, "But you can't carry up there. Why would you go to a country that doesn't let you carry your gun?" My response was, "I don't need one. The people are civilized, and it's safe." It fell on deaf ears, and once again, my friends smirked, chalking it up to the socialist influence of my Canadian wife.

As we wheeled away from the border in Buffalo, I remembered seeing an outdoors store along the Interstate a few miles back. I quickly punched it into our GPS unit and decided to drop my pistol off there. I wanted to have a Crimson Trace laser sight installed on it anyway, so I thought this solution was a stroke of genius. I presented the gun at the front service desk where the security guy attached a bright red zip tie through the chamber, indicating there were no rounds in the gun and it was safe. As I made my way back to the gunsmith, Jill took the opportunity to check out some warm wool hiking socks. I knew she was pissed, but as is her way, she sensed I felt like shit too, and she didn't want to hurt my feelings and didn't mention how stupid this whole scene was.

I rang the buzzer on the gun counter and out from the back came a short, wire-haired guy wearing a shop apron. He smelled like pepperoni pizza and gun oil.

"Can I help you, Bud?" he said.

I placed the pistol on the soft mat on top of the glass case.

"Hi, ahh yeah, can you guys install a Crimson Trace on this little Ruger? I want to drop it off and come back for it…"

He interrupted me.

"Nope. No can do. That gun's not legal here, and if you leave it I have to report you," he said.

"You need to get that pistol out of this store, Buddy! Now!"

I picked it back up and immediately put it into my coat pocket.

Wow! I had no idea. I guessed the magazine capacity or the short barrel length or something was against the law in New York.

My heart immediately started racing, and sweat began to run down my forehead under the wool cap I was wearing. I swallowed hard and saw my future choices either behind bars in Attica State Prison, or creating an international incident at the Canadian border. My thoughts can be overly dramatic when my big brain is under stress. I tried to breathe and think this through calmly.

I did an about-face and marched double-time towards the door. I passed Jill.

"Honey, we have to get out of here, NOW!"

"But I'm getting socks…" she said.

"No. Come with me. Let's go. NOW!"

I may have over-reacted, but with the close call at the border and now the gunsmith on my case, I felt like a gun runner or something. What the fuck was I going to do with this gun? I thought of throwing it into the Niagara River, but it was expensive, and my favorite carry-pistol in Florida. It was small yet powerful—the perfect concealed carry gun for warm weather and light clothes. But this wasn't Florida anymore, Toto. This was gun-control-central, and I was running around with a banned firearm.

When we got back to the van, it took me a minute to compose myself. Then Jill came up with a good idea.

"Can you ship it home to yourself?"

Damn. She was right. We found a post office, and right before it closed, grabbed a flat rate Priority Mail box and ran back out to the van. I stuffed the box with the gun, magazines, and ammo, and, being a bit paranoid, to help disguise it from x-rays, I put some carabiner clips, Jill's cave diving helmet, and a few little hand tools into the package. I wrapped them all in a beach towel, taped up the box, and ran back inside to mail it home. I must have looked nervous when the clerk asked if there was anything hazardous or dangerous inside, but she took the box. I paid my $12.50, and the evil gun was out of our hands.

We made our way back to the border, and the whole time I am hoping that there aren't any loose rounds, or a stray magazine or anything that a Canadian border guard's dog would alert on if we got searched. I was also creating a scenario in my head where the New York State Police got tipped off by the gunsmith and had radioed ahead to Canadian officials to warn them that a gun smuggler in a big white, windowless van was running for the border. (As if they don't have more important things to do.) As Jill pulled up, she presented her Canadian passport and my American one. The only two questions the woman immigration officer asked was, "Are you two married? You have different last names." I tried to hold pleasant, neutral eye contact with her - that's what the professional smugglers in the movies do, right? Of course, we answered yes we are married, and she then asked where we were going in Canada.

"Home for Christmas in Toronto with my family," Jill said.

The border officer smiled, saying, "Ahh, that's nice. Have a good visit."

She waved us on, and my heart stopped beating a mile a minute. I reached over and squeezed Jill's hand.

"I love Canada, honey."

"You haven't seen anything yet," she replied. "We even have nicer jails for gun runners, and according to Ricky and Julian - they have great food, and allow conjugal visits at Christmas time."

She was making a clever reference to characters from the Canadian comedy series, "Trailer Park Boys." It is, apparently part of the citizenship test to know about this, "Red Green," "The Tragically Hip," and other pop culture icons.

I bit my tongue. I deserved it.

Because I grew up in a big northeastern American city, guns weren't part of our upbringing. We didn't hunt for deer, or fish, or shoot skeet or anything like that. The few men in our neighborhood who hunted usually went out on a week-long trip to upstate Pennsylvania sometime around Thanksgiving. There was a tradition among some of them to grow a beard beginning November 1st, and to not shave it until after the hunt. I guess it made them feel a bit more feral inside. If you've ever seen the movie "The Deer Hunter," that was close to what these guys experienced - especially the part about Rolling Rock beer, "From the glass-lined tanks at Old Latrobe." But, on a row-home city street with about 65 families, only two men had ever hunted. As a child, I only saw guns fired on TV, and in real life, they were secured in shiny leather holsters, slung on the hips of soldiers and police officers.

The first time I ever touched a real gun was at Navy boot camp. We carried around old M1 Garand parade rifles all day. These were real military rifles, but had the firing mechanisms removed, to prevent incidents or accidents. Another movie reference comes to mind: "Full Metal Jacket" in which a disturbed Marine recruit causes havoc with live rounds and his boot camp issued weapon. I fired my first gun at the shooting range during the middle week of basic training. It was a .22 caliber pistol, at an indoor shooting lane. Big deal, I know. A peashooter compared to weapons I'd later handle. But for a city kid like me, any gun was so foreign in my hands that just getting the rounds to hit the paper was an accomplishment. I did well and put all 24 bullets into the black circles. I even scored a few bull's eyes.

The next time I touched a firearm was about six months later. I was at Navy Seabee combat training at the Army's Fort Ord in California. This time it was for real. The Seabees are combat engineers, and as such, they are often deployed right beside U.S. Marine units to help support the Marines with combat construction capability. The Seabee motto is "We Build, We Fight." This also applies to them off duty: "We Build, We Fight, We Drink All Night!" Instead of a ..22 pistol, I was issued the first-line infantry weapon of the day, the M-16 A2 rifle. The M-16 is the granddaddy of the current AR-15 and other scary black rifles. It fires the .223 round, and several generations of this venerable firearm have seen action in combat over the past few decades. After a week of intense training, I earned the "Expert Rifleman" designation and was awarded a shiny medal for wearing on my uniform. For the next 15 years, whether attached to active duty or reserve military units, I earned multiple expert ribbons with both rifles and pistols. Not bad for a street kid from Philly.

There were a few occasions over those years where I checked out my weapon from the armory and was deployed to active combat. I was never involved in a close-range firefight but did experience a few times where enemy bullets whizzed over my head. I was glad that I could take apart and re-assemble those M-16's while blind-folded. (Yeah, that's really a thing in the military. Usually, a semi-inebriated competition involving bragging rights, side bets, and shots of Jack Daniels.)

I was also trained on and familiarized with the M-60 machine gun, M-203 grenade launcher and LAW shoulder-fired rocket. If ever a private citizen was qualified to own personal firearms, it was me. When I first applied for a concealed carry permit from my local Florida sheriff, I didn't even need to take the mandatory training courses. My military records reflected my expertise, and the sheriff waived the class requirement and issued a card immediately. This was in the early 90s,' and now it is a bit more complicated, requiring more paperwork to get a concealed carry permit. But without a doubt, military veterans are favorably considered. Overall in the State of Florida, the law is worded as the sheriff "Shall Issue" a gun permit to any adult citizen who takes the classes, fires a few rounds down range afterward, and is not a domestic abuser, sexual offender, convicted felon, or otherwise certifiably batshit crazy. That's it. And believe me, many of the people I know who carry guns should not even be trusted with a pocket knife or pair of scissors. I can't imagine them being able to respond appropriately in a stressful, life or death situation without either killing themselves or an innocent bystander. For fuck's sake, even experienced law-enforcement professionals shit themselves when confronted with deadly firepower. I can't see a typical, half-blind, glaucoma-glasses-wearing, retired Florida grandpa drawing his Glock and successfully shooting himself out of a gas station hold up. I'm afraid there would be wounded bodies strewn everywhere.

Some of my best friends and acquaintances don't dare leave the house without strapping on a gun. And this is not exclusive to men. There was a small party I attended in High Springs, and the conversation turned to "who might be carrying?" A very informal survey of about 25 people turned up 18 firearms. Five of them were women, including a middle school teacher who claims to carry her pistol every day into her classroom. And, this is in what used to be a pretty safe community, mostly small towns and rural farms. However, in the previous two years before this party, there were four major shooting incidents nearby. In one, a father got into an argument with his son over a pickup truck's parking space and killed the son and his wife with an AK-47 rifle. That happened six miles down the same road on which I lived. In the second incident, a grandfather went nuts and fatally shot three of his grandchildren and his daughter when they got off the school bus at the end of his driveway. That happened about nine miles away in the next small town. A third incident involved a local policeman in shooting a man as he tried to snatch his grandchild from her stepmother outside the local school. With an AR-15 pointing at him, the officer had no choice but to shoot and kill the grandfather. And most recently, two Gilchrist County deputies were ambushed and murdered while eating lunch in a local diner. The shooter has not been found. All these events occurred within a 15-minute drive from our home.

In Florida, a private citizen can, with proper permitting, carry anything from a small single-shot Derringer to a .50 caliber Desert Eagle semi-automatic pistol tucked into the waistband of their board shorts at the beach. They can carry a gun at the grocery store, Walmart, the gas station, just about anywhere. The exception includes bars and pubs that sell alcohol. And schools. Yes, schools. Oh, the schools.

Schools throughout the United States are very soft targets for anyone who wants to wreak havoc. Yes, some, but not most, have a police presence. In Florida, the place with which I am most familiar, a lot of county school districts assign a deputy as a "Resource Officer" to a few schools in their area. But even with this officer present, some schools have been successfully attacked by gun-wielding mass shooters.

On February 14th, Valentine's Day 2018, the armed and trained school resource officer assigned to Parkland's Marjory Stoneman-Douglas High School in Broward County, Florida, remained hidden outside the as the massacre of students took place just a few dozen feet away. The deputy never engaged the shooter. The deputy never entered the building. The good guy with a gun did not stop the bad guy with a gun.

I was recovering from knee surgery and working at home during the day that this attack happened. Jill was teaching a class with her cave diving students a few hours away in the Florida panhandle. Like some other newsworthy events, I first noticed something was up when my Twitter feed began to scroll at high speed. I went to some breaking news websites and saw the incident unfolding in real-time on social media. When all was said and done, seventeen people lay dead, and seventeen others were seriously wounded. The perpetrator, Nikolas Cruz, was a former Stoneman-Douglas student who was captured several hours later after eating at McDonald's then walking through a Walmart store. He used an AR-15 rifle to mow down his helpless victims, most of them his former classmates. Yes, the same AR-15 that is the civilian version of the M-16 I carried in the military.

By the time Jill came home that evening, she had heard reports of the shooting on the radio. When we finally had time to process what had happened just a few hours south down the highway, we were both in tears.

"Are you okay honey?" I asked.

"No, Robert, I am not okay!" she said.

"I will never be okay with kids being murdered in schools. What is wrong with America?

Our house, at this time, had six of my guns spread across several rooms.

In the depressing hangover of the most recent school shooting, I said, "Maybe we should think about accelerating our plans and live full time in Canada?" Jill had always intended to move back home, but I was reluctant to leave my American comfort zone permanently.

Jill has dual citizenship. She moved to Florida in the late nineties to pursue a career in scuba diving and media; a career that is a bit more challenging in her icy Canadian waters. Jill tells me that she has never, ever identified as American. I have always considered her as purely Canadian. She even speaks with that peculiar "Bob and Doug MacKenzie" Ontario accent.

After Parkland, we got acutely serious about moving to Canada and put our American house on the market. I think we were mentally prepared to live in Canada and before we even had a buyer for our Florida house, Jill and I purchased a small condo in a small town on a river outside Ottawa. It was a great deal, and we figured it would be our summer place until our Florida house sold. (I know this is backward. Most people my age retire from Canada to Florida.) It was the cold-blooded Stoneman-Douglas mass slaughter that pushed me over the edge. I was so upset and angry that my country's political class did nothing but offer "thoughts and prayers" as innocent children were again being mowed down at school. I could not thrive in a place that condoned this. As I watched the news coverage, a wave rushed through me: This is what America has become. If this is acceptable, I could no longer continue to live in the United States of Donald Trump. My dream of a better country was dead and buried beside the innocent Parkland high school kids in the graveyard of reality.

I got very depressed. I was taking oxycodone to manage the physical pain from my recent knee replacement surgery, but it didn't help much with the emotional pain I felt. The Parkland slaughter tripped a panic switch for me. I became desperate to get the hell out of the cesspool of America before it circled down the drain for the last time. Parkland changed everything.

Once again, innocent people were shot down like animals. Once again, the shooter was not supposed to have access to firearms. (The shooter had a well-documented behavioral and mental health history.) What was happening in America? What was happening to Americans where so many people could come to accept our schoolchildren being slaughtered regularly? After the Columbine massacre 19 years earlier, I was confident that American society would tighten access to guns. I thought, (and wished) that American politicians would grow some balls and stop cowtowing to their National Rifle Association contributors. But, nothing of consequence ever happened to change the culture, and more frequent shootings occurred. The Columbine shooters were marginalized as violent, video game playing goth kid misfits who listened to Marilyn Manson music. After a few months, the Columbine shooting fell into the dustbin of history as a shocking anomaly, and the conversation turned from actual gun control to a rating system for popular music and first-person video games. Thank you Tipper Gore. It took Michael Moore and his documentary film "Bowling for Columbine" to jumpstart the gun control conversation. But, sadly, Moore was, pardon the pun, "out-gunned" by the NRA and their money machine. He was painted as an enemy of freedom and the 2nd Amendment, while, in reality, he was a long-time Michigan hunter and Life Member of the NRA. Smeared as a communist, anti-American agitator, Michael Moore, whom I respect and admire, didn't have the resources or political gravitas to fight the NRA. In my opinion, America would be better off with a few million more agitators like Mr. Moore.

Although the Parkland shooting proved to be the last straw that galvanized my desire to leave America, it was only one of many mass shootings that wore me out emotionally over time. Before Parkland, it was Sandy Hook.

A few weeks before Christmas, 2012, in Newtown, Connecticut 20-year-old Adam Lanza entered Sandy Hook Elementary School and killed 20 six and seven-year-old children. He also murdered six adult staff members and his own mother. Lanza used his mom's AR-15 as his primary weapon. Sandy Hook was the beginning of the end for me. I knew I wasn't going to remain in the United States if there was not a real effort to remove guns from the hands of the millions who should never have them.

Americans seem okay with mass shootings, and they have shockingly become routine events. I can't accept this.

Mass shootings and senseless violence are not the only pressing issues engulfing America. With Donald Trump as president, there will continue to be nothing but chaos and criminality coming from his administration.

I know this isn't the first time you've heard this, but the United States is about to have some severe cultural, economic, and political catastrophes. The election of Donald Trump and his extreme right-wing friends is just the tip of the iceberg. When the economy melts down, and it will, Trump and his 1% criminal class at the top will do fine. But, Joe Six-Pack is going to feel pain like never before. Wall Street cannot possibly continue on such a bullish path, and when it crashes, it will be global. The well-paid manufacturing jobs are gone, and they aren't coming back, no matter what Trump promises at his latest narcissistic rally. The student loan crisis is going to burst, especially when the public discovers that their educational loans have been chopped up and bundled into derivatives, just as the mortgage markets were a decade ago. People with outstanding student loans are going to be in shock when the private investment firms that bought their loans begin calling them in. Professionals like doctors, engineers, and computer scientists are going to be filing bankruptcies left and right, only to discover that their student loans can't be discharged and they are essentially going to forfeit every asset they think they own to pay them off. And it is not only young people with loads of debt who are going to see their financial world popped like a balloon.

Retirees with union and corporate pensions are going to go to the well and find it dry. Gasoline prices will shoot to astronomical levels, and only the wealthy or corrupt will freely travel. The food train will come to a slow grind. The shelves at the grocery store where you currently shop only carry about 3 or 4 days worth of stock, and when the farms fail due to climate change, and truckers can't afford the gas to transport what little harvest there is, parts of the country will find themselves in the unbelievable position of mass food riots. It will resemble Mad Max more than the Home of the Brave. I know this may be unthinkable to most of you, for now. Just ask your cousins in Puerto Rico or New Orleans' 9th Ward if such a scenario is fact or fiction. Go to Flint, Michigan, and try to find a clean drink of water. Unthinkable in 21st-century America.

Donald Trump and John Bolton might have us in a hot war with Iran in a matter of months, and the country will be even more divided. War with Iran will not be easy. Iran, or ancient Persia, has one of the most capable military forces on earth. The American people, for the most part, don't have much of an appetite for war, but Trump doesn't care. He only caters to about 32% of the country that adores him. His cult will follow him to the gates of hell if he asks them. And he will. That is one of the points of the endless rallies. He is shoring up his "street team."

Add to this mess the festering tribal conflicts that already exist between the races, sexes, and religions in America. And then, for good measure, let's throw in a few million guns.

According to a 2017 report in the Guardian (UK), there are at least 265 million guns in private hands in the United States. And of these, almost half are owned by just 3% of the population. Look around at a hundred people in your neighborhood or your job. Now, imagine that only three of these people own all the guns. In a real emergency do you think they will help you? Are any of those three the type of person who shows empathy, kindness, or generosity? Are any of the three amongst the smartest, most skilled people in your group?

I didn't think so.

It is highly probable that the three people who own the guns are much better prepared for the crisis at your doorstep than you are. They may have been prepping for a decade, waiting for this time, the day the shit-hits-the-fan. Likely, these three people are not in a sharing mood. It is probable that when you reach out to them, they will shoot you rather than help you out, claiming that you came to steal their stuff. (This exact scenario just happened in the aftermath of Hurricane Michael in Panama City, Florida.) Why will they shoot you? Because they can. Because they have all the guns. Because law enforcement will be absent. Because it will be the law of the jungle. Because they simply can and will. And they probably have a rack full of red MAGA ball caps.

If Donald Trump is still president when this moment-of-truth scenario begins, he will declare a national emergency and initiate martial law. It will be strongman Trump for the near future in America. And, in case the crisis doesn't arrive before he is about to leave office, don't be surprised if he and his loyal bootlickers manufacture some event that triggers this nightmare scenario. I've been warning my naive friends of "The Resistance," that Donald J. Trump intends to be president-for-life. He will not voluntarily leave the White House. If he loses his bid for a second term, Trump will claim the election was rigged. For those who were paying attention, he began to plant this seed during the 2016 presidential election. Even Hillary Clinton is hinting at this possible scenario. The recent 2018 mid-term ballot fiascos in Florida have set the table for just such an occurrence. (Why is it always Florida?) Trump's aversion to the rule of law is evident. Who, exactly, will force him from office if he loses an election? Who, exactly, will frog-march him from the oval office if he is impeached and convicted? Will "The Resistance" wearing their pussy hats parade down Pennsylvania Avenue and demand his ouster? Trump's armed-to-the-teeth "Deplorable Brigades" will likely meet them. Yes, Mr. and Mrs. Apathetic America, it will be your second Civil War, and the bloody outcome will change the United States forever.

Not exactly my American Dream. I'm going to go out on a limb and say it isn't yours either.

But, I don't despair.

I am the most fortunate man in the world. I got to fall in love with and marry the smartest, kindest, and the most remarkable person I ever met. I never knew that loving another person could be so wholly joyous and liberating. When Jill entered my life, I became a better man. She challenges me to this day to be the best Robert I can be. I can only hope that I do the same for her. We took a solemn vow to each other to "never have a boring day," and a dozen years down the line, we have upheld that promise. (For example, I am writing this from the cabin of a ship sailing through an iceberg field in Antarctica).

It is vital that we don't let the turmoil in American politics and culture become embedded in our psyches. Jill and I have a peaceful space where we can be creative and live our fullest lives. Our spirits are not broken by the bedlam that emanates from Washington, D.C.

We have made our move. We now live full-time in Canada.

Making Our Move

The move to Canada was not as easy as I thought it would be. I miscalculated how far along in recovery from my knee replacement surgery I would be. Still using a cane to walk, I was not much help getting what few things we still owned after our moving sale into the back of a U-Haul truck, let alone drive it to Canada. Cas, one of our good friends from Newfoundland, volunteered to help with the move. He used his air miles to fly down! He really saved my butt, and by sharing the driving with Jill, he gave us travel options. By the way, every single person from Newfoundland you spend more than ten minutes with will become your greatest friend. Newfoundlanders are the most friendly, thoughtful, and fun people you will ever meet. So, the journey began: Jill and our friend driving to our Canada place while I flew into Ottawa with a bum knee.

I had been coming and going from Canada for a few years in the summertime. Jill and I escaped the oppressive Florida heat and lived in unusual domiciles like a houseboat on the Humber River in Toronto, and a seasonal trailer near Waterloo's Mennonite Country. Each time I had entered Canada, I simply handed the border guard my passport and, after a few routine questions, was on my way. But, this time, coming into Ottawa airport, it was different. I was nervous. This time I was flying in alone, on a U.S. passport that was only valid for six months. Yet, I intended to make Canada my permanent home. What would I do if I got turned away? I no longer had a home or belongings south of the border. Jill was in a truck somewhere between Florida and Canada with everything we owned. There was no turning back. I was sweating it when I walked up to the Customs booth for questioning. The Canadian border officer took my passport, scanned it, asked what my business was in Canada, and if I had anything to declare. With a determined voice, I said, "No, nothing to declare just visiting family in Ottawa." Then he waved me on with "have a good stay." That was it. I guess I masked my nervousness, and I was in! (I had a backup plan. Jill's brother lives in Ottawa, and I had all his contact information at the ready in case the officer's probed deeper.)

In a few days, Cas and Jill showed up at our condo, and with a burst of energy, we emptied the U-Haul and walked across the bridge to celebrate our new beginning at the local craft brewpub.

I was here in Canada. I was staying. We did it.

The process of becoming a permanent Canadian resident is a lot more complicated than I imagined. There are mountains of forms, both paper and electronic, to fill out. There is a requirement for an FBI background check and a police letter. There is an extensive (and expensive) medical exam. Most of all, a whole lot of patience is needed while waiting for a response from Immigration Canada. We paid almost two thousand dollars upfront, just for the privilege of applying for permanent residency under the family category. For my American friends, this is the Canadian version of a "Green Card." It is the first step towards becoming a Canadian citizen. If all goes well, I will eventually have dual U.S. and Canadian citizenship.

We began our online application in late May, as soon as we had our condo set up. Holy shit! What evil poutine-eating sadist designed this process? At almost every point of the application document, we ran into nearly impossible requirements. They needed everything, including my grade school information, military service records, employment background, foreign travel receipts…you name it. They wanted me to document my friggin' life for the past 60 years! Frankly, I used to drink heavily and have entire decades I can't recall, let alone document. I have an ex-wife who burnt all our marriage records in some New Age "purging of the soul" ceremony. Now, Immigration Canada wants to know all about my previous marriage. The first night Jill and I went through the forms together, I wondered whether our current marriage would survive the process. We definitely saw things differently. I wanted to gloss over many of the requirements, but Jill, who is a stickler for accuracy and follows the rules, insisted that I take time to reach back into my oh-so-non-conformist life and answer everything thoroughly.

"You have to think of this as a long term project, Robert," Jill said. "We are working on the rest of your life as a Canadian, and that's worth doing correctly. Mistakes and omissions will get flagged and only slow us down anyway."

She was right, of course.

There weren't enough spaces on the forms to list all the places I've lived and worked over the past forty years. I have not exactly led a traditional life. I realized a long time ago that my short attention span and problem intellect weren't a good fit in a straight job. Even after earning a nursing license, I approached my career in a very mercenary manner, working as an independent contractor and traveling nurse. I worked when and where I chose, accepting thirteen-week assignments at interesting places with mild weather. If Immigration tried to research my nursing jobs, they'd run into dead ends. Some of the hospitals where I did short-term staffing gigs no longer existed. On almost every page of the application, I had to scramble to find paper records.

Many people have all their essential documents neatly filed in a fireproof metal box. My life's filing cabinet resembles more of a dumpster fire. Outside of my military service, on paper, I just looked like a wandering hobo. My lack of permanence wouldn't look good on my application. I was ready to quit the whole thing several times, but Jill, the eternal optimist, continued to encourage me to practice some patience and keep working at it. And work at it I did. It took three months to research and gather all the required documentation. The most agonizing experience was obtaining an FBI background letter. It was another expensive and drawn-out process. We had the entire application completed except the FBI letter. There was no way to predict how long the FBI response would take. Some people receive their documents in three weeks, and others take three or four months. I sent in my request both online and by U.S. snail mail. Then we had to wait. And wait. At long last, almost three months later we had our FBI letter! What we began in May was finally finished and sent in at the end of August. For several months after mailing Immigration Canada all the application paperwork, there was radio silence from their end. The only thing I had to prove they received my application was a receipt from Canada Post saying the package was delivered. Patience is not one of my strong characteristics, and every day, for months, I checked the progress of my application at the Immigration website, only to become more frustrated with the lack of communication.

As a visitor from the United States, I was only allowed to stay up to six months in Canada. I arrived in mid-May, and as the months passed and we heard nothing about my residency application, I was getting anxious. By late October, I had only weeks left. I asked Jill for guidance.

"What should I do?" I said.

"Don't worry. Just apply for an extension. You're my husband. They won't come and kick you out of the country. It will work out," she said, in all her optimistic Canadian glory.

Well, I am more of a skeptic, and very little of Jill's optimism has rubbed off on me over the years. I applied for the extension, and, again, didn't hear anything. So I was preparing Plan-B: Jill had eight weeks of work in the U.S., and I'd accompany her. I would return to the States for a short time, and when I came back up to Canada, my six months visiting status would reboot itself. Seven days before my visitor visa expired, I crossed back over the U.S. border into New York. After a brief stop in Cleveland, where Jill had a speaking engagement, I was sitting in a camper trailer in north Florida. It felt weird to be back in America.

After six months in a small Ontario town, with a slower pace and quiet neighbors, America just seemed way too fast, way too loud, and way too big for me. It was like returning from a remote expedition, or a long military deployment. My PTSD was immediately triggered by the large crowds, aggressive drivers, and rude personal interactions. While waiting for Jill to check-in at the hotel near Cleveland, a cab driver rolled up next to me, beeped his horn and lowered his window. As I rolled down mine, he started cussing me out, screaming like a madman about how I cut him off a mile back with the small camper trailer I was towing. His blond mullet framed a red face with bulging eyes. The veins were popping out of his neck. He punctuated his rage by slamming his fists into the steering wheel of his road-weary taxi as he yelled expletives that made Jill blush. It had been a while since I've driven in the U.S., and I was a little dumbfounded. There was a time when I would have jumped out of my car and pounded the guy into next week. But, after so much time in Canada, my first instinct was not to be confrontational. I said, "yeah, sorry, I didn't see you." Wow. Maybe Jill's Canadian optimism has rubbed off on me. But back in America, I had to recognize that the crazy cabbie was probably packing a pistol. For the rest of the trip I decided to be very careful while driving, and that discretion was indeed, the better part of valor.

Hanging around a Florida campground while Jill was diving gave me ample time to take inventory of where I stood in this crazy space between two countries that sometimes seemed like two different worlds.

A big part of my anxiety about gaining legal status to remain in Canada had to do with observing the deteriorating political environment in the United States. Looking down from the North, I've tended to be more detached and less emotional about the dire situation. But, I am an empath. I can't help but feel other people's pain. When I see injustice and corruption, it gets all over me. All my life, I've had an innate sense of fair play. And, I feel a particular responsibility to try to right a wrong. It is the way my father raised me. I stood up to bullies. I offered help to people who were worse off or weaker than me. When reasoning failed, I was known to punch my way through a few righteous street fights. Jill describes me as a former Philly tough guy with an overactive brain and a sensitive soul. The world can be hard and cold, yet I've always found a way to move forward honestly and without stepping on others.

Throughout my adult life, I've witnessed the demise of the American middle class. Since the nineties, I've noticed fewer people enjoying upward mobility. I've seen jobs go away and never come back. I've seen hard-working, middle-aged men and women laid off at Christmas time and never get called back to the plant again. I've seen the mills, factories, suppliers, and services in entire small towns disappear. Looking at upstate Pennsylvania, or small-town Indiana, you'll see the rusted hulks of a once-prosperous middle-class society crumbling to the ground. These places are the hometowns of real people who played by the rules, worked hard, and invested in the American Dream. Their dreams turned to dust as the world's economy globalized, and digital technology advanced at a pace so fast they couldn't keep up. I remember seeing a television news segment about the changing realities of the new economy. The presenter interviewed middle-aged, unemployed auto workers who were retraining in a computer science class. The premise was that they'd learn to program the very machines that were replacing them on the assembly lines. Unfortunately, the programmable robots and machines were in Mexico and China, and just a half-dozen programmers could keep an entire factory buzzing twenty-four hours a day. Over time, most of the men and women dropped out of the classes and either received some form of government assistance or accepted any low wage job they could get. I am sure those people had different life plans when they first landed the good union jobs at the auto plant. That's why I always try to be kind to older Americans who are still in the workforce. They are not bagging groceries in their twilight years because they want to. That grocery store job might be the difference between eating a well-balanced diet or barely surviving on cheap cat food.

Here's the truth: "The Powers That Be" consider middle-class people expendable. The career politicians sitting in Washington and at State Houses have lied to, deceived, and yes, robbed working folks for decades. Members of Congress, Senators, Legislators, and presidential candidates show up every election season promising to rebuild these hard-working communities. The pledge to bring them back to the prosperous places they once were. They vow to "make them great again." Then, after the votes are counted, the same lying, cheating, corrupt politicians retreat to their security-fenced townhomes and McMansions, forgetting about the very people who voted them into the lavish, powerful lifestyle they enjoy. It is frustrating to watch the will of The People ignored. Only well-connected lobbyists and wealthy campaign contributors have access to the seats of power. This is not what I would call representative democracy.

So, how did such a corrupt outlier as Donald Trump win the presidency? He campaigned on a promise to throw a monkey wrench into the gears of the big government machine that stole the jobs, foreclosed on the houses, and most of all robbed the dignity of decent American working people. He sold himself as a political outsider who would go to Washington and "Drain the Swamp." He assured them he'd build a wall to keep Mexicans from coming into America and stealing their jobs. He stoked fears about murderous immigrants smuggling drugs and raping their daughters. Somehow, this unapologetic scoundrel, this New York billionaire con-man, convinced everyday Americans he was one of them, and that he alone understood their plight. They thought he was the Alpha and Omega, the only one who could miraculously fix their broken lives. They lined up to attend his rallies. They bought his stupid, made-in-China MAGA hats. They put up yard signs and plastered bumper stickers on their pick up trucks. Then, on election day they all marched out to the polls in MAGA battalions and voted against their own best interests.

Many of these MAGA voters were my north Florida neighbors who could not be swayed by my argument that Trump was a low-life fraud who wanted to use the presidency to enrich himself and his family - a position I easily backed up with reason and facts. Like the well-meaning guys at Doug's garage, most Trump voters were voting emotionally. They despised Hillary Clinton with a passion. They were angry and frustrated with the status quo. In the ultimate irony of ironies, many Evangelical voters believed that Donald Trump was ordained by God to lead America back to the path of righteousness. As an agnostic-pragmatist, I saw this as childish magical thinking. Just because Trump expressed support for the State of Israel and promised to move the American Embassy to Jerusalem, religious Christians looked beyond his adultery, corruption, and lying. Maybe some of them held their nose as they voted for him, but they helped a bonafide heathen ascend to the most powerful office on God's green earth.

The presidential campaign of Donald Trump may prove to be the biggest crock-of-shit in American political history, but his campaign strategy worked. It worked bigly.

So, there I was, reluctantly stuck smack in the middle of Florida Trump Country. There were still MAGA political signs on people's lawns. They hadn't removed them since 2016. I even saw a few homemade "Trump 2020" signs painted on sheets of plywood and adorned with little American flags. (No doubt the flags were made in China, too.) In almost every diner or gas station in the southern province of Redneckistan, there was someone with a MAGA hat or a Trumpian slogan on a tee-shirt. Do you remember the guy from south Florida who was charged with mailing pipe bombs to prominent Democrats and news organizations? Did you see his van, covered in right-wing Trump propaganda? Slap on a few Bible verse decals and magnetic Christian fish, and these "Jesus-mobiles" are more common than one would think down south. In one of the poorest, most depressed regions of the United States, the locals have not grown weary of all this "winning."

I visited Doug's garage during my second week back in America. Only Doug and his retired friend Tim were there.

Tim was keen to show me his new toy - a short-barrelled .223 machine pistol with a laser sight and scope. It looked like a miniature version of an AR. When he pulled it out of a leather rifle scabbard placed between the console and passenger seat of his dusty old Chevy, I was taken aback for a moment. Man, such a powerful weapon, so casually carried in the family car was something I hadn't seen in a while.

"Here, Robert, take a look at this little baby," Tim said.

He handed me the mini-rifle. The muzzle was pointed right above my head.

"Shit, I'm not sure I want my fingerprints on this thing, it can't be legal," I said.

"Nope, the ATF says it is as legal as any other pistol. Any semi-auto," Tim answered.

"Well, you should know," I said. "You've been on the ATF's list for a long time."

I took the weapon and pointed the barrel away and down at the grass. I released the magazine and held it up to inspect it. There were full metal jacket rounds in it. I pulled back the charging handle. A round popped out and bounced under the vehicle. Sure enough, Tim had a live round in the chamber. I should have known better.

"Fuck, Tim! You didn't even clear this thing before you gave it to me? Christ dude, you're the real Florida Man. You know, the guy who shoots his friend's dick off while showing him a gun. For fuck's sake Timmy, unlike you, I'm still using my dick, so maybe you could practice a little bit of gun safety?"

Doug snatched the gun from me.

"Goddamn you Tim. Don't be an idiot." Doug scolded.

"Gee Rob, I guess you've turned into a gun pussy since living in Canada," Tim said.

Yep, that's me. Robert the gun pussy. Back in Florida, I wondered about buying a new pistol to carry for the duration of my visit. A "Florida Gun." It had been years since I walked around unarmed in America. I still had a concealed carry permit. But, as Tim says, I'm a "Gun Pussy," so…no. Besides, if anything stupid happened, and I got caught up in some shit while carrying a gun, I could pretty much kiss my chances of ever being allowed into Canada goodbye. It was a hard choice. I felt a responsibility to provide security for Jill and myself, but I guess my little pocket knife would have to do. Without a gun strapped on my hip I was becoming a lot more conscious of my surroundings. I gave people plenty of leeway. I lost the desire to aggressively enforce the social contract or meddle in anyone's business. I minded my own, keeping my head down, and just biding my time until I could return to my quiet Ontario town to be with all the other Canadian gun pussies.

Are we Americans are so fucking scared of each other that we need to carry the firepower of a Navy SEAL every time we drive over to the grocery store?

MAGA vs. Resistance

Right before our return to Florida, the 2018 midterm elections resulted in a Democratic Congressional landslide. They would soon be the majority in the House of Representatives, but the Senate would be in the hands of Republicans. So, a split Congress.

The most encouraging result, in my opinion, was the number of women and minorities who would be seated in the House. I have long believed that if women ran the United States, it would be in much better shape than it is now. The budget would be balanced, we'd have free and fair trade with most other nations, and we wouldn't be involved in endless wars. We might even enjoy genuine universal health care and affordable higher education. You know, like the rest of the civilized, developed world. Like Canada.

I have heard first hand from men who refused to vote for Hillary Clinton because they believed that a woman was not qualified to be president. And yet, they voted for, and continue to support Trump, who has no idea how the presidency or the rest of the government works. They selected an egotistical braggart with zero diplomatic, government, or academic experience over a former First Lady, Senator, and Secretary of State. I think that Hillary's education and experience intimidate some men, and that is the crux of the issue.

If you are a man and have never had a strong, smart, independent woman in your life, you are missing out. I am fortunate in that Jill is all of these things. She is a recognized expert in her field. Despite being one of the few women working on a project, she is often in a leadership position on the expeditions she undertakes. Her technical underwater missions involve sophisticated life support, and that means simple mistakes can be fatal. There is no room for error, and her team depends on her good judgment and experience to survive each dive. If you are the kind of man who feels threatened by women holding and exercising power, you may need to examine your prejudices. You're probably not the macho beast you pretend to be.

In the mid-term elections, I voted on the Florida ballot. I chose the most progressive candidate in each case. I voted for Andrew Gillum for governor, Bill Nelson for the Senate, and other Democrats for all the other positions, from dog-catcher to the State House. Florida had some interesting ballot initiatives, and I chose the most reasonable positions; from restoring voting rights to former convicts to ending greyhound racing. And, as I have recently become accustomed, most of the candidates I selected narrowly lost their races. Overall, Gillum was a fantastic candidate, but couldn't overcome the active Republican base organization in Florida. I think we will be seeing Mr. Gillum on the national political stage in the years to come. Nelson, on the other hand, was a very lukewarm candidate. Yes, he is a hero astronaut and a fairly decent person, but he is firmly established as one of the career Washington politicians that populist Floridians have been railing against. I think his time has come and gone. If the Democratic party had run a more youthful, progressive and enthusiastic candidate against Rick Scott, (For example, Mayor Gillum), they might have picked up a Senate seat.

Except for some rare pockets of progressive-minded voters in Gainesville, Tallahassee, Tampa, and Palm Beach, Florida is very much a conservative state. But it is changing. The numbers are beginning to even-up, and in a few years, I can see Florida transitioning into very liberal progressive place. But, the "Old Dixie Dogs" continue to dominate, especially at the state and local level. Just look at how gerrymandered the voting districts are, and you can see there is a great effort to break up the liberal minority voting blocs. Republicans in Florida's State House can feel the warm progressive breath on the back of their necks, and they are doing everything they can, legal or not, to retain power. I predict that the 2020 general elections in Florida will be so corrupted that if Donald Trump loses his reelection bid here, he will refuse to accept the results and attempt to retain power by all means necessary, constitutionally or not. He will challenge the electorate, call the results "fake news" and insist that voting was rigged. The sad thing is that he will make such claims, not in a legitimate court of law, but in a Twitter tirade. And if his case ever gets to the Supreme Court, his recent Justice appointments likely will tip the balance in his favor.

At the grassroots level, Florida is a potential MAGA powder keg. There are hundreds of loosely organized, well-armed groups and militias loyal to Trump. If he loses an election, the Trumpian cult members will transform from being merely annoying and obnoxious, to violently opposing the legitimate defeat of their Dear Leader. Yes, I said, "cult." The seeds are being sown, right now, in small back yard gatherings and giant arena-sized rallies, where

Trump whips his blindly loyal base up into rabid, frothing MAGA Regiments.

With the possibility that the Democratic majority in the House of Representatives will begin impeachment investigations into Trump, I sense a certain kind of desperation among his most devoted followers.

During our Florida trip, I tried to gauge the temperature among the Trump loyalists at Doug's garage. The mood among the men at Doug's who fervently follow Trump is more disturbing than ever. I use the word "follow" rather than "support" because his disciples are steadfastly committed to him, right or wrong. It doesn't matter. They have ceded their free will and have morphed into brutish devotees of his cult of personality. They have become so emotionally invested in Donald J. Trump that they are sure to respond with violence when he gives them the not-so-subtle signals. One need only look back at his campaign rallies where he incited his crowds to fisticuffs against protestors to see evidence of this.

"Timmy, what are you going to do when Trump is impeached or indicted?" I asked.

"Oh, don't worry, there are plans already. You wouldn't want to be in D.C. when that shit goes down," he answered.

"So, you are going to arm up and march on Washington?"

"It won't be a march, bud. It will be a tactical occupation of the swamp." Timmy said.

Tim is a slothful, grossly-overweight man in his mid-sixties. He can barely walk from his vehicle to the overhead door at Doug's shop without wheezing and getting out of breath. I couldn't see him making a pilgrimage to "occupy" Washington.

"So you are talking revolution?"

"Call it what you want, Rob, but when we are finished, there won't be much of a Deep State left standing," Tim said.

"So you will be committing treason, right?" I asked.

"It isn't treason when you are taking out the Shadow Government," Tim continued. "We are going to go up there to remove the real treasonous pricks. We the People are the Patriots, not Pelosi, Obama, Hillary - not any of them are true Americans."

Wow, Timmy had been listening to way too much Alex Jones. He spends a lot of time on extreme right-wing web forums, and this is the message they are parroting in every corner of white America: Trump is the white man's salvation. He is the last, great white hope. If you support

Trump you are a patriot; if you oppose him, you are an anti-American liberal suffering from "Trump Derangement Syndrome" and deserve to be in a re-education camp. No middle ground. They cling to Hillary's Benghazi debacle, Podesta's Pizza Gate, and Barack Obama's Muslim Brotherhood loyalties as if they were facts. The weirdest right-wing, wack-job conspiracy forums are also pushing threads about young Michelle Obama's male to female sex change. Yes, that's right. I find it hard to take anyone seriously who contributes to these conversations. But Tim lives and breathes this shit. He's even a moderator on one of the darker forums that is extremely popular with the hardcore end-times survivalists.

It is talk like this that scares the shit out of me. I am convinced that if and when Trump is voted out or legally removed from office, there will be an uprising among the white supremacists, evangelicals, and right-wing militias.

I intend to be observing this constitutional crisis from my safe haven in Ontario, Canada. And it will hurt me deeply because there are people that I care about who will act stupidly in such a futile effort on Trump's behalf. And Trump couldn't give fewer shits about these people who are willing to be his cannon fodder as he pursues greater personal wealth and power. There is no reasoning with these people. I've tried it with Tim and the other the guys at Doug's. They are prepping for the Great White Insurgency.

I think that advocating armed revolution does not make one tough, and it should certainly not be tossed out as half heartedly as Tim throws it around. It doesn't give a man character - in is an indictment of his character. It says that civilized reason and thought are too difficult. We are at the point in history where, for some people, their go-to reaction to unjust society is violence. Violence is easy, but it doesn't usually accomplish lasting goals.

The recent election of so many progressive, activist Democrats is somewhat promising; however, I'm afraid the mid-term Democratic gains in the House may prove to be too little, too late.

Christmas in Antarctica

Jill and I spent Christmas, 2018 in Antarctica. It was one of the fantastic things I have experienced as the husband of an acclaimed Canadian explorer. We flew to Ushuaia, Argentina, met a ship, and sailed across a stormy and unsettled Drake Passage to the icy continent. The ship, RCGS Resolute, is a partnership between the Royal Canadian Geographical Society and One Ocean Expeditions. It is part research vessel and part adventure expedition ship. On Christmas Day, we ferried inflatable Zodiac boats to a sheltered inlet where we walked carefully among penguins and seals. Here's a scoop for you: both penguins and seals smell like shit. Real shit—one of the most pungent odors I have ever experienced. (And I spent years living with nasty sailors in the Navy). But, as I took in my extraordinary surroundings, standing on an ancient polar glacier that meets the turquoise sea, I realized that despite the earthy stench of the most feral creatures on the planet, it was Christmas Day, and I was standing on fucking Antarctica!

From the Zodiacs, we observed giant humpback whales swimming under and around us as they fed on krill and small fish. If you ever want to feel insignificant in the grand order of the Universe, venture out into the Southern Ocean on a 15-foot inflatable rubber boat as some of the most magnificent creatures on the planet breech the surface and blow just a few feet away. There were a dozen of them, males, females, and juveniles, and our little boat must have seemed like a bathtub toy to them. It was exhilarating and a little bit scary at the same time. If one of these giants tipped over our boat, we would not last long in the frigid water. The whales are 50 feet long and weighed 30 tons, yet they were some of the most gentle and graceful beings I'd ever seen. There is an intelligence in their eyes, and I find it abhorrent that some cultures still hunt them commercially.

We witnessed nature at its most raw and unfiltered when we saw a pod of Killer Whales teaming up to prey upon penguins. The frantic penguins swam underwater like little torpedoes, then popped up unexpectedly on the surface while the Orcas tossed the poor, flightless birds up in the air before snatching them with their razor-sharp teeth. It was a humbling experience to be a helpless human in such an untamed environment. One thing was certain; people could never survive here for very long without technology.

Antarctica is a neutral continent, governed by a treaty promoting conservation, research, and peace. There is no industry, resource extraction, or nationalism. The area is divided into giant wedges of territory containing scattered research stations that are staffed by scientists from various nations. The most populated and well-known research station at McMurdo Sound is administered by the United States. Presently there are about 1300 people working and studying there. During my Navy days, my Seabee battalion shared a headquarters building on the base at Port Hueneme, California, with the Navy's Antarctic Development Squadron Six (VXE-6). These were the operators that flew the specially equipped C-130 aircraft and handled logistics for the U.S. Antarctic Program. I was offered a transfer to the unit in 1988, but declined, because, well, Antarctic winter. Wintering over at the South Pole was not even on my radar in those days. But, here we were, decades later visiting the region at Christmas (which is Spring in the southern hemisphere). We took an opportunity to drop in on the Chilean Antarctic research base. The dozen or so scientists and air force personnel seemed very happy to see us. They even set up an impromptu post office so we could purchase postcards and have them postmarked from their official Antarctica mailbox. Sending a postcard from Antarctica to Ontario costs less than five U.S. dollars. I don't think Canada Post could beat that.

A side benefit of our amazing polar trip was that we were very much cut off from the news of the outside world. There was very spotty, expensive, and infrequent satellite Internet service on board the Resolute. Logging on was a tedious process and in many ways reminded me of the early days of dial-up Internet. I remember the process of inserting a precious AOL disk into my P.C.'s slot and after a few minutes of beeps and buzzes, getting connected to the World Wide Web. Magic! That is until my older sister picked up the telephone in her bedroom and disconnected me from the line to the server. A fantastic, digital world was just at its infancy in those days. Who knew that only a few decades later we'd all have smartphones and be able to check email from Antarctica. For a price, of course.

This holiday season news blackout and digital detox helped knock back my anxiety over Donald Trump's ruination of my native country. It was getting to me before we left. It seemed like every! Single! Goddamned! Day! There was another Trump-instigated-event that pushed America to the brink of catastrophe. When the Trump administration, (are there maybe four dozen people left)? And Congress could not agree on a budget that included funding for his much-touted border wall, so the Federal government was shut down just before Christmas. I chalked it up to the usual .gov dysfunction that we have all seen before. In a few days, most of us figured, they would come to some kind of compromise and the federal workers would be grateful for an extended holiday break. And when an agreement was reached, everyone would dust themselves off and get back to work. But wait, this was Trump's America, and he managed to run this train right off the rails. We were thirty days into this debacle with no end in sight. Federal workers were about to miss their second paycheck.

Returning to Canada by air, we were lucky to avoid American airports. All of our connections were in Argentina and Brazil before we came through Toronto to Ottawa. Trump's shutdown had made the situation with unpaid TSA staff at U.S. airports less than pleasant. The security queues were becoming tortuously long, and passengers were missing connections. Rank and file TSA workers were never among the highest-paid civil servants in the federal system. The beginning salary is about $26,000 per year, or to put it in perspective, about half the average pay of the manager at your local McDonald's restaurant. The minimum wage for a high school kid working at the grocery store where I now live in Canada is $14 per hour. That equates to about $29,000 Canadian, which is pretty close, factoring the exchange rate, to a TSA screener. It was always troubling to me that the only people standing between the next 9-11 hijacker and me were overworked, underpaid cogs in Big Brother's grand Patriot Act scheme. Unable to afford the gas to drive to work, thousands of unpaid TSA workers were simply calling in sick, compelling those who could make it to the airport to cover their shifts and work unscheduled overtime with skeleton crews. I really felt for them, but I am glad we didn't have to go through their screening process this time. Donald Trump and the millionaires and oligarchs he runs with down at Mar-a-Lago don't have any idea about what's it's like to suffer barefoot and belt-less through TSA screening lines.

I have worked for the federal government. Besides my military enlistments, I was a nurse in the V.A. Medical System. I spent a few years employed at V.A. hospitals in South Dakota and Florida. As a disabled veteran myself, it felt like a noble calling. But, I also found it to be one of the most dysfunctional environments I've ever worked in. There was rampant corruption in the V.A. administration at almost every level, even the local hospitals. Contracts were awarded based on bribery and kickbacks. Employment positions and promotions were almost exclusively decided on a "who you know" basis. The meritocracy was overshadowed by nepotism. Waste, fraud, and abuse were the ground-rules of nearly every department. A "use it or lose it" budget process encouraged supervisors and department heads to spend millions of taxpayers dollars needlessly, fearing that if they didn't, the next fiscal year's budget would be cut or curtailed. I remember being told to use unbelievable numbers of IV fluid bags because the stock at our hospital was "over sufficient." Only a U.S. government nursing supervisor would use a phrase like "over sufficient." Where I come from, it simply means we have enough, and we won't run out. She claimed we needed to move it out to request a higher number of cases for next year. We were instructed to only run 400-500ml of each 1000ml bag before unnecessarily replacing it and changing the tubing sets out on the orders of our charge nurses. We were told that if anyone asks, just say you think the tubing may have been contaminated, so you are practicing good infection control techniques. I refused to do it and was accused of not being a team player. If other federal agencies operated anything like the V.A. Medical Centers, it is no wonder the government is bloated and inefficient. This waste, fraud, and abuse has been the grounds that the extreme anti-government types always point to when they call for abolishing federal departments and agencies. There is this weird political faction in the United States that walks the edge between libertarianism and anarchy and would like to see the federal government reduced dramatically. They subscribe to the philosophy espoused in a 2001 NPR interview by right-wing thought leader Grover Norquist: "I don't want to abolish government. I simply want to reduce it to the size where I can drag it into the bathroom and drown it in the bathtub." They also like to quote President Ronald Reagan, who, in his first inaugural speech of 1981 said, "...Government is not the solution to our problem; government is the problem." However, Reagan's statement is out of context. He was specifically addressing the solution to the economic recession he inherited, not making a blanket statement about government in general. God knows, Reagan didn't have a problem with big government when it came to military spending, or increasing the budgets of the departments which he held dear. He, like today's Republicans, sought to lower taxes on the rich, and cut programs and assistance to the poor and underprivileged. (That's kind of been the GOP playbook for decades now.)

I served on active duty in the Reagan era. When deployed, we had everything we needed and more. My battalion acquired new equipment and supplies at a breakneck pace. We didn't have Seabees that were trained to operate the latest equipment, but it sure looked pretty sitting unused in the yard down at Alpha Company. Then, after Reagan, Democrat Bill Clinton became Commander-in-Chief and began closing down unnecessary military bases and cutting antiquated service units. We suddenly had to practice a little responsible budgeting. Reagan's gravy train came to a halt and Clinton initiated the Base Realignment and Closure program. (BRAC.) So, I have seen both responsible and wasteful government spending at the grassroots level. I can only imagine what those numbers look like up at the top of the government food chain; they must have many more zeroes in them than I ever encountered or was responsible for.

In the middle of the 2018 government shut down, some voices of the right were calling for altogether abolishing the furloughed worker's positions. They reasoned that if these government workers are so non-essential that they could not be called in and forced to work without pay during the shutdown, maybe their positions should be eliminated. Or perhaps we could take Grover's advice and drown these greedy, useless bastards in the bathtub?

There was a time, not so long ago, I'll call it the "Pre-Reagan" era when an honest job with the federal government was a ticket into the prosperous middle-class for many Americans. Geez, just a job as a janitor at the federal level meant decent pay, full medical, retirement benefits, and lifetime job security. But somehow, Americans were brainwashed into thinking that a janitor, or a clerk, or a maintenance worker didn't deserve a stable middle-class paycheck. They were coaxed and conned by the Rush Limbaugh's of the world that lower-skilled positions were only deserving of poverty wages. After all, many of the unskilled federal workers were minorities and just a little on the brown side. And, worse, they tended to vote for liberals and Democrats. So, little by little, piece by piece, the federal civil service system that hired blue-collared people was dismantled. Instead of offering decent pay and a government job, hiring was contracted out to corporate vendors. And, of course, these contractors were friends and campaign contributors to politicians of all stripes. Democrats, Republicans, and everyone in-between had a hand in this. In the name of austerity (though they would prefer to use the more positive term "privatization"), contracts were handed out to those corporations and companies that were in favor. And guess what? Many of the lower-skilled positions are, under the contractors, either eliminated or given to undocumented immigrants who work for pennies on the dollar. I mean, what does it take to clean the bathrooms at National Parks? How essential can that worker be? Oh, that's right, they are shut down. However, people are still using the parks, and the shitters are broken and overflowing. I'll avoid the obvious Trumpian analogy I could insert right here.

Most Americans would be shocked to find out just how many essential government services are provided by contractors. When I was in the Navy, we had our own Mess Specialists - sailor/cooks who managed our kitchens. Today, giant civilian contractors like Haliburton or Wackenhut run the mess halls and supply just about everything else from beans to bullets. Many federal prison guards are no longer government employees but are on the payroll of Corrections Corporation of America. And, truth be known, they are paid less, with fewer benefits than their government counterparts. During the recent shutdown, many contractors were not being paid, so it is just a matter of time before they started calling in, claiming they couldn't afford to put gas in their cars to get to work. The sad thing is, unlike the federal workers, they had no guarantee that their jobs or back pay would be there for them when they could finally afford to return.

One of the saddest realities of the recent shutdown was the discovery that many federal employees who missed one paycheck were unable to make mortgage payments, put groceries on the table, or pay for their children's daycare. A CNN report claimed that many Americans had less than $400 in cash reserved for a financial emergency. I was shocked!

During the shutdown, I heard Donald Trump say that federal employees should be able to "make arrangements" with landlords to pay back rent and other overdue bills. This is a guy, who, besides coming from a family of New York slumlords, I can reasonably surmise, has never written a rent check or paid a residential light bill in his life. Hell, it is well-known that Trump stiffs contractors, vendors, and almost anyone else with whom he does business. And, apparently, he is trying to run the federal government just like he runs his businesses, right into the ground.

Hopefully, the Democrats in Congress can slow this out-of-control presidency down. Nancy Pelosi may be the person to do it. She has a better understanding of how government actually works than anyone in the Trump administration, including the President himself. Pelosi is a master politician and a tactful negotiator. Trump hung his entire presidency on the ridiculous idea that he was going to build a wall across the southern border, and get Mexico to pay for it. Nancy Pelosi said, "Nope." And, unlike her presidential nemesis, I think that Pelosi means what she says, and says what she means.

The fact that millions of Americans think it is a good idea to build a wall to keep out migrants who are trying to get to America to better their children's lives makes me very sad. Frustrated and disappointed may be a more accurate description. I always thought America was better than this. Besides all the 21st-Century arguments about technology that make this 8th-Century wall a stupid idea, I believe that the hateful, racist, bigoted views that a wall represents are more damaging than the actual structure.

The United States and Canada share the longest open, non-militarized border between nations in the world. I cross it regularly with my U.S. passport and a wave from the border guards. However, if Trump is re-elected in 2020, I'm driving over to Ottawa and asking the Canadian Prime Minister to consider erecting a big, beautiful wall, steel barrier, or moat with polar bears, from New Brunswick to British Columbia.

Either that or I'm signing up for research duty in Antarctica.

Baby, It's Cold Outside

"Baby, it's cold outside." This mantra has been my earworm for weeks now. Let's talk about cold. Like, really, really cold. Bone-chilling, dick-shrinking cold. This may not be news to many of you, but in wintertime, Canada is a frigid place. We moved from north Florida to a small town near Ottawa, in what can only be described as an ass-backward way for a sixty-something-year-old guy to plan his later years. As I walked down Bridge Street, the main street in my new town, in the depths of December, I noticed it was 32 below zero Celsius. That's minus 25.6 in 'Merican. (At those temps, the .6 doesn't even count). Thirty-five kilometers north, in Ottawa, the news outlets and Twitter feeds were proudly proclaiming that the city was the coldest Capital in the world. Colder than Ulan Bator in Mongolia. Colder than Moscow in Russia. Colder than Astana, Helsinki, and Reykjavik. I'll remind you that Reykjavik is in Iceland, and there is a reason the country is named "Ice"- Land.

Because I am married to a fresh air loving Canadian woman, she decided at minus 32, it would be a good day for me to learn how to walk in snowshoes.

"Honey, the snow on the trail today looks perfect for snowshoeing," she said.

"There is no such thing as perfect for anything outside in December," I said.

"No, really, Robert. If you are going to be Canadian, you have to learn to be outside all year' round. Otherwise, you will get old and stiff from lack of movement."

"I already am old and stiff," I said. "Maybe we can accept that fact and stay inside where it is warm?"

I was ten months out from my total knee replacement surgery. There were many days when I didn't feel like moving much because of the pain, nerve tingles, and stiffness, but Jill would insist that I cycle, walk or stretch. And, every single time, she was correct. I always felt that I achieved a small orthopedic victory, any time I was actively out in the world. And she was right again, so I went snowshoeing.

"Holy shit, I can't even get these things on!" I said.

"Take your time. They are not complicated. Let me help you." Jill said.

"No!" I have to learn how to do this myself," I grunted, as I struggled to slip the straps over my toes.

We were standing in shin-deep snow next to the trail. I was already hating it. The bindings and straps were, indeed intuitive, but I managed to get them reversed. I was just about to say how proud I was of myself to be able to bend and stretch and reach down in my puffy parka to put the snowshoes on when gravity and physics intervened. Splat!

"Shit! Shit! Shit!" I said. "I just fell into the snow with both hands and no gloves on! Oh shit, my fingers are already frozen!"

Jill just laughed.

"Not funny! I said. "You are the one that is going to have to carry me home and drive me back to the States so I can thaw out at V.A. hospital in Florida!"

"Honey, you're doing fine for your first time. Just slow down, and do one buckle at a time," she coaxed.

Because Jill is a living, breathing Saint on this Earth, she knelt and cinched the last strap I was struggling with, and helped me retrieve my gloves from the snowbank.

"Okay, follow me at your own pace," she said.

Now, on my best days, Jill walks about half again as fast as I do. Everyone in her family is tall and lanky, and they are from a lost tribe of "giant striders." They walk all the time. After every meal I've ever had with her 85-year-old father, he decides he needs to walk a few miles, leaving me in the dust. She got that from him. I've always known that Jill is hard to keep up with intellectually and physically, but I try not to let it intimidate me. She's an exceptionally strong, athletic woman.

"Jill, can you slow it down just a notch, please?" I begged.

"Oh, I'm sorry, am I walking too fast?" she queried.

"No, baby, I'm walking too slow. Actually, I'm sliding along with tennis rackets strapped to my feet."

Not my most graceful moment.

Then, suddenly I stopped thinking about walking, and it just seemed to click. We humans tend to overthink most things, and I am the King of the Land of Over-Analysis. When I just let my body move naturally, it worked. I realized that the snowshoes performed better in the deeper snow. When I walked along the edge of the groomed trail, in the virgin snow, the tennis racket-shaped contraptions kept me upright and moving forward. Easy-peasy. I was feeling more Canadian by the minute!

If there is one observation about Canadians in winter, it is that they don't let the weather dictate their lives. When it snows, they ski, snowboard, or do cross country on the trails. Most towns of any size have plenty of public facilities for indoor activities as well. Our little town of 11,000 has an indoor swimming pool, a sizable hockey arena with two rinks, open ice skating, several youth hockey teams, and a half-dozen private membership gyms. There is a brand new curling club, because not only is curling an athletic endeavor, it facilitates drinking alcohol and moving one's body simultaneously. If you'd rather exercise your brain, the town has a modern library with great selections and public access Internet, community centers offering all sorts of lectures and hobbyist clubs, and even the town hall has a beautiful public auditorium featuring an eclectic schedule of stage plays and live concerts.

It is difficult to resist comparing winter life in Canada to the cold weather lifestyles I experienced in the United States. In Canada, the main street shops are busy, even in the harshest weather. People make an extra effort to patronize small, family-operated businesses along Bridge Street. Also though there is a new Walmart out on the highway that skirts town, many people avoid it. We do too. One of the requirements we insisted on before we decided where we would live in Ontario was that it had a vibrant town center. The ability to leave our condo and walk to our bank or to the Post Office, or to grab a cup of coffee at an independent local cafe, is a luxury we rarely found available in the States. It seemed that in Florida, even though the weather was mild, we drove everywhere. The towns were designed for cars, not people. We tried bicycling as much as possible to run errands or make grocery runs, but just getting on the bike and going to Winn-Dixie for our basic needs was a 20 mile round trip on hot, treacherous roads with angry motorists. And there were few if any bike lanes or sidewalks. Many years ago, I read James Howard Kunstler's, "The Geography of Nowhere," and it made a lasting impression on me. In the twenty years since I read that remarkable book on urban planning and town design, I've been seeking to live in a place designed for people, not automobiles. To be fair, this town is very old and was laid out before the car was invented.

The place was settled in the early 1800s by Scottish and French colonists on what was indigenous Algonquin and Wendat territory. A fast-flowing river promoted the construction of mills along the banks. (We live in a former grain mill, converted to modern condos). The mills brought the railroad and eventually the highways and byways to connect these industrial factories to the rest of Canada. I give great credit to the town's leaders, who, over the years recognized the value in preserving the historical heritage and aesthetic beauty of the old stone buildings, and did not raze them in favor of modern steel and glass. This place feels like a village; a community knitted together by a common core. Although the English and French influence are strong, like the rest of Canada, this is an increasingly diverse region. For my American friends: there are non-white people here who live, work and prosper. They may have come from the Middle East, Asia, or Africa, but today, they are Canadians. And most of the marginalized minority cultures that are shunned in America are accepted and celebrated here. This little town has a Pride Festival every August, celebrating our LGBTQ neighbors. When I fill out forms at Service Ontario, the gender section includes female, male, and "non-binary or other." There are dozens of same-sex married-couples living regular, routine lives in our town. I chalk it up to the absence of fundamentalist Christian churches.

The Church, although an essential part of many people's lives, just isn't given the same influential platform here as it is in the United States. People's religious beliefs and practices are a mostly private affair in Canada. In the time I've lived here, not a single person has asked me what religion I follow, or has invited me to their church. Contrast this with one of my first business meetings in Florida where, at the outset, I was asked which church I belonged to, because that's how business influence is measured down there. (The meeting was about a music festival, and it opened and closed with the Baptist Pastor leading us in prayer.) In that part of Florida, you have to belong to the "right" church, the accepted denomination to get any business done. To get over the awkward Christian hurdles at that meeting, I answered with an imaginary church: Saint Jill of the Pines, named after my wife. I got away with it because there are hundreds of small family congregations in that Florida county that enjoy tax exemption by erecting an outbuilding on their property and declaring themselves a "Church."

Many churches in Ontario are also community centers, with all sorts of activities and classes. The United Church of Canada around the corner from us offers everything from Tai Chi and Yoga, to Alcoholics Anonymous and Girl Guides meetings. Somehow, I never saw a Christian church in my former town in Florida offer Yoga or, God forbid, Tai-Chi. Why those are heathen practices and Jesus, who apparently fasted and meditated often, would never approve!

In Florida, many people don't know the names of their closest neighbors. They live in gated communities designed to keep certain undesirable people from having access. They live behind bars on their windows and doors. They create home prisons in which they feel safe from intruders who might come to take their stuff. They arm themselves against the threat of strangers who might invade their space. Floridians created legislation like the "Castle Doctrine" and "Stand Your Ground" laws that exonerate them, should they murder an innocent person who dares to trespass upon their hallowed, deed-restricted and neatly groomed lawn. Not long ago there was a billboard on I-75 south as you entered Florida reminding tourists that Florida was a "Stand Your Ground" state. It was a creepy warning that citizens had the right to shoot and kill you if you dared trespass on their lawns. The sign didn't stay up very long. I think the Florida Tourism people had a problem with the message and pressured the outdoor advertising company to remove it. This heightened paranoia is simply an unimaginable concept to most Canadians. I searched online and looked in several community newspapers and could' t find a single business in Ottawa that will install bars over your windows. This is the capital city of Canada, and if you include Gatineau, across the river in Quebec, there are about a million people living here—people who don't fear their neighbors to such an extent that they feel they must erect walled-in, private housing developments, or put steel bars between themselves and their fellow citizens. We often leave our back door unlocked when we are out on a walk through town. (If you do come in when we are not here, could you clean the place instead of stealing our laptops?)

I'm slowly acclimatizing to winter. I'm noticing that I am wearing fewer layers of merino wool while in the house. I'm also venturing outside more often, regardless of the temperature. When I recently walked to Canada Post and the grocery store in minus eighteen temps with wind-blown snow, I wanted Jill to give me a Polar Medal upon my return. She didn't. Instead, she gave me a warm cup of tea and a pair of down-insulated camp booties to wear indoors. So, equipped with our all-wheel-drive Subaru, dressed in layers and layers, and wearing an expedition parka while becoming proficient with snowshoes, I just might make it here. I'm a little shy about getting up on ice skates though, for now. The city of Ottawa is intersected by the Rideau canal. In winter, the frozen canal is turned into the world's largest outdoor skating rink. For several kilometers, the water is drained to a lower level and allowed to ice over, creating a winter playground for skaters. Some people commute to work on skates with briefcases and backpacks slung across their bodies as they glide into the office. A year ago, I would have thought this was crazy, but now, it seems normal.

Oh, my God! After just a few months of winter here, I am turning Canadian! Okay, Baby, maybe it's not so cold outside - if I stay active and know how to dress for it I might make it through to Spring.

Christchurch

After ten months of living in Canada, my increasing anxiety about the political situation in the United States became somewhat manageable. The Trump administration's scandals and the growing chasm between disparate groups of Americans seemed less dire when viewed from north of the border. Maybe because in our house we were not tuned to twenty-four-hour cable news, the klaxon alarms warning of the imminent Trump dictatorship seemed a little less distressing. I don't use the word "Dictatorship" lightly. Just recently, at a public event organized by Trump's handler Steve Bannon, a seething middle-aged American woman stepped up to the mic and forcefully proclaimed: "Never in my life did I think I'd like to see a dictator, but if there's going to be one, I want it to be Trump." Led by Mr. Bannon, the crowd stood and clapped.

This is how it begins.

Our freedom-fries-loving-friends and neighbors, who fear Mexicans and other brown people, have become susceptible to Trump's cult of personality. I am afraid for them. They are so deeply invested in Trumperism that they can't possibly turn back now. It would be admitting they were patsies who were taken advantage of by one of history's most notorious con-men. Even if, deep inside their hearts, they know they made a huge mistake, they must deny it. It is hard to admit when one makes a mistake publicly. Lord knows I've made plenty in my life. However, the first step towards recovering from my numerous errors was admitting them in the first place. It is not so easy for the MAGA devotees. As Trump assaults democracy, replacing it with his corrupt autocracy, his followers will blindly follow. Like lemmings, they will be led off the cliff, and as they plummet into the morass, they will think they are "winning" because Trump told them so.

I know that when America sneezes, Canada catches a cold, but the level of trepidation over everything Trump says or tweets seems a bit less desperate up here. Recently, Justin Trudeau, the Canadian Prime Minister, found his government caught up in a scandal connected to SNC-Lavalin, a huge Quebec construction firm. Compared to the Trump scandals, the SNC Affair, where Trudeau's office allegedly tried to influence the Canadian Justice Minister's treatment of SNC, seems like small potatoes. It would hardly be a blip on the radar of the corrupt American political topography. But, in Canada, a nation where ethics and fair-dealing is expected of government officials, showing special treatment to a particular corporation, no matter how many good-paying jobs they provide, is considered wrong. It is refreshing to live in a place where a sense of right and wrong is baked into the mainstream social fabric.

My regular intake of American political news is limited to nightly YouTube streams of CNN, "The Rachel Maddow Show," and Stephen Colbert's funny, yet politically-charged monologues. I find Colbert's humorous take on the day's events to be a more accurate and valuable analysis than many of the professional political pundits. Sometimes I need a good joke to get me through the reports of the United State's imminent collapse. One of the barometers at my disposal in measuring the seriousness of the day's news is how long Jill can remain awake during Maddow's show. If the reported situation in America is not yet at the red-alert level, my wife will usually fall asleep within the first ten minutes of the program. (Sorry, Rachel.) This leaves me to fend for myself, hoping that as I doze off, the nightmare that is the state-of-the-world does not keep me from a restful night. But, all-too-often, it does.

One night, as Jill slept peacefully beside me, I watched the live stream, and as Rachel finished explaining the latest legal wrangling of the Mueller investigation, I surfed through a few more YouTube channels. One of my "go-to" online channels for breaking news is "Agenda Free TV." A guy called Steve Lookner runs a one-man Internet news operation from a small home studio in Atlanta. As news breaks around the world, he live streams the story, moderating discussions, and replying to Tweets and Facebook comments. Lookner is a likable anchorman with a valid, "fair and balanced" approach to reporting. He sources his online content responsibly, soberly delivering urgent news. Just as I was about to turn off the screen and go to sleep, Agenda Free TV put up a breaking news alert. There had been a shooting at a Mosque in Christchurch, New Zealand. Needless to say, I didn't get to sleep for a few more hours.

I popped open my laptop, and as Steve Lookner pieced together the latest bad news on our bedroom smart TV screen, I searched the #Christchurch Twitter feed. It didn't take long before an auto-play video of the gunman slaughtering dozens of innocent Muslim worshippers splashed across my timeline. The images were horrible. The gunman had strapped a camera to himself and recorded his brutal execution of women, children, and men in the mosque. As he walked into the building, he blasted a few men at the entryway with a semi-automatic shotgun. When the shotgun's shells were expended, he tossed it aside and swung an AR-15 rifle into position, and moving from room to room, mowed down terrified, defenseless people as they huddled together and scrambled to find any kind of cover they could. The shooter circled back to previous areas and finished off the wounded as they lay bleeding on the floor. It was later reported that the perpetrator streamed the killings on the Facebook Live platform. I was disgusted that people were posting the stream all over social media. This is the world we live in today. Everyone is digitally connected. A few minutes after a dreadful mass murder occurs on the opposite side of the globe, I can watch the gruesome act from the safety of my comfortable bed. It looked like a first-person shooter video game, except the blood spraying onto the walls was real, and the lives extinguished were living, breathing, valuable human souls, not some animated fantasy characters.

As the night wore on and more facts became known about the New Zealand shooter and his motives, it was reported that he was captured alive and arrested. Before his rampage, he had created a lengthy, rambling manifesto and posted it online. The 29-year-old Australian shooter stated in his manifesto that he subscribed to the White Supremacist ideology. He hailed U.S. President Donald Trump as "a symbol of renewed white identity and common purpose." He wrote the names of white power icons, and he drew supremacist symbols on his weapons and ammo magazines. Investigators revealed that he had been espousing his views and threatening violence on Internet forums like 8 Chan.

As I followed the story, the grisly details broke my heart. My faith in humanity sunk a few more notches. Man's inhumanity to his fellow man is something I will never understand. What kind of feral beasts roam amongst us? Is this really the best we as a species can do? Such repugnant acts all too often reinforce my disappointment in humanity. I wanted to wake Jill and seek some comfort in her warm humanity, but I consciously didn't disturb her. I didn't want these terrible images to be the last thing she sees before she goes back to sleep. There was a time, not long ago, when such an event as this would have been such a shocking anomaly that waking my wife would be justified. But no. Now, our society has become so sick, so mind-numbingly brutal, that the murder of fifty innocents in a house of prayer didn't even warrant CNN to interrupt its 24/7 Trump bashing marathon to report the atrocity at Christchurch in real-time. I'd let Jill sleep. I reached over and felt the soft skin of her arm and thanked my stars that we live a blessed life of privilege, love, peace, and tolerance.

Maybe I'm an idealist, but I had hoped that by 2019, the world would be a more intelligent and charitable place. I felt despondent as I watched the New Zealand shooting unfold. But, as awful as it was, I think I am becoming a bit calloused to the world. When the Parkland school shooting happened, I was heartsick for days. I cried, I shouted at the TV news. I sought unanswerable answers. I took Parkland personally. I saw it as a new low point in American history. But, after the mosque shooting in New Zealand, I was a bit annoyed at myself because I was becoming desensitized to the frequent shootings.

As bad as Christchurch was, I can't say that it surprised me. The Western bigots, some of whom sit in influential positions, have been subtly advocating for violence towards those who don't look or pray as they do. I saw and heard it among my friends, the guys at Doug's Garage. Some of them constantly referred to practitioners of Islam as "Muzzies, Mudslimes, and Sand Niggers." The men at Doug's have never knowingly spoken to or interacted with an actual Muslim person in their lives. But, easily influenced by right-wing talk radio, Fox News, and shadowy Internet forums, my buddies, bought a first-class ticket on the Xenophobe Express. I am relieved that I don't live among them anymore, but feel ashamed that I accepted their bigotry for so long. I'm sure that some of them admire the mosque shooter and commend him for taking direct action on behalf of white culture. Plus, the shooter used some serious firepower, and semi-autos give these guys a gun-boner. I am too weary of arguing with such Neanderthals. Yes, I am very thankful that I am in Canada and don't live among these knuckle-dragging, mouth-breathing morons.

The world has been segregating itself into primal political, ethnic, and religious tribes for centuries. In this technological age, it is easy for malleable people to be recruited to extreme causes. In my mind, there is little difference between a fundamental ISIS extremist and the zealots who show up at the Dear Leader's rallies wearing MAGA hats.

Donald Trump, when asked the day following the Christchurch massacre if white nationalism is a growing threat, said, "I don't really, I think it's a small group of people that have very, very serious problems, I guess."

Every time this man opens his mouth, the United States of America loses whatever is left of the moral authority it once wielded in the world. When people ask me why I left Donald Trump's America, sometimes it is hard to communicate clearly how much the declining morality was a factor. The American society in which I was raised, the American Constitution to which I once swore to protect with my life if necessary, has been so corrupted by Trump and his supporters that I no longer consider the current United States as a valid representation of the Republic the Founders created.

Donald Trump is not "Making America Great Again." He is creating a new degenerate America. A fourth Reich. An America for the white, the wealthy, and the obedient sycophants who do his dirty work. The most shocking thing is discovering that these sycophants are both at the highest levels of the executive branch, and my former friends and neighbors.

Civics Lessons

I've often wondered why I am such a political junkie. One would think that when I decided to leave America, I would leave my infatuation with American politics behind as well. It turns out I was imprinted at an early age.

When I was in second grade, maybe seven years old, our class studied American History. Because I went to a Roman Catholic school in Philadelphia, the American Revolution was part of our local story as well. When we learned about the Declaration of Independence, we took a field trip to 5th and Chestnut streets and explored Independence Hall. Back in the sixties, Independence Hall and the immediate area around it was not yet managed by the U.S. Park Service. The buildings that made up the historic site were minor tourist attractions in need of repair. The historic site was absorbed into downtown Philadelphia, surrounded by office buildings and brick townhomes, and was hardly the remarkable tourism focal point that it is today. Independence Mall provided a bit of green space in the middle of high-rise urban development and at one southwest corner, it connected diagonally with a small park known as Washington Square. Arriving on smoke-belching old school buses, we were herded over to the square where we ate box lunches on shaded picnic tables beside the monument dedicated to the Unknown Revolutionary War Soldiers. Our teacher told us that the square was once a cemetery where soldiers, both English and Colonial, were buried during the war. I was careful to walk only on the paved pathways through the park. I didn't want the bad luck that I was sure to accrue from stepping through the grass and on to an unmarked soldier's grave. I felt creepy knowing that bodies were laying six feet below where I was wolfing down a ham and cheese sandwich. After lunch, we marched across Walnut Street and filed into the dank-smelling, damp hallways of Independence Hall. The first thing I noticed was that the interior of the building was smaller than it appeared in paintings, movies, and history textbooks. The long hallway leading to the Liberty Bell had meeting rooms on each side. Its floorboards creaked, and some of them had old nail heads sticking up. The grand staircase should have crowned the artifact, but the noble Liberty Bell sat unpretentiously in the dusty shadows. Local historians, acting as volunteer guides permitted us to go into the very rooms where the Declaration of

Independence and the United States Constitution were debated and adopted. We touched the dark, aging chairs in which George Washington, Thomas Jefferson, and Benjamin Franklin once sat. The "Rising Sun" armchair from which Washington presided during the adoption of the Constitution was still in its original spot at the front of the room. Apparently, Ben Franklin observed the ornately carved sun on the back of the chair and said, "I have often looked at that behind the president without being able to tell whether it was rising or setting. But now I know that it is a rising sun." Running my little fingers across the carved relief of that sun, gave me a weird tingle of excitement. The shiny silver inkwell, in which the Founders dipped feathered pens to sign the Declaration of Independence, sat on the wooden desk placed on a small riser at the front of the room. I sensed, even at such a young age, that something very significant happened here. The guides and teachers spoke in reverent tones. They whispered, scolding us as we strayed into the few little nooks and crannies adjacent to the main rooms. I recall long, green velvet curtains that blocked out all light and ventilation from the big windows. It was a warm spring day when we visited, and the interior rooms of the Hall were hot and stuffy. I wondered if the Founders, with horse shit on their boots, dressed in wool clothing and lacking personal hygiene, stunk up the joint on their way to Independence. That's what a sweaty seven-year-old thinks of in the ultimate shrine to American freedom.

Most of what the tour guides droned on about was a little over my head. The Continental Congress, the State House, the first U.S. Capitol… none of this really sunk in. I was not as interested in the mundane facts as I was in awe of walking the same worn wooden floors that the giants of American history had tread. I remember the guide pulling the velvet ropes aside and allowing us to take turns sitting in Jefferson's chair. The seat was well-worn, and my skinny butt only filled half of it. My feet barely touched the floor in front of me. The importance of the moment, sitting in the very seat that Jefferson occupied as the United States was born, has stayed with me all my life. Decades later, when I stood in ranks to be sworn in to the U.S. Navy, raising my right hand, I took an oath to "Support and defend the Constitution of the United States…" I recalled my second-grader-self, sitting in Jeffersons chair. Every time I think about that field trip, I can still smell that stuffy unventilated room, where enlightened men created the most advanced form of self-government ever known.

Over the course of my childhood, I had the opportunity to visit Independence Hall many times. My father had a keen interest in American history and occasionally took me to walk the streets around Olde Philadelphia. We'd start at Independence Hall and walk down to the docks on the Delaware River that once was the mooring of the fledgling Continental Navy. We'd get ice cream at a storefront next to the brick building that housed the first United States Post Office and the printing press upon which Benjamin Franklin produced the Poor Richard's Almanac. Tagging along with my dad, I'd skip over the cobbles of Elfreth's Alley, the site of Betsy Ross' house and the oldest continually occupied residential street in America. We'd go past the homes where Continental Statesmen and European Generals once stayed as they carved out the New Republic. When Dad wanted to teach me about the drafting of the Declaration of Independence, we'd go stand on the corner of 7th and Market streets, where Jefferson once rented a two-room apartment as he penned the historic document. Living in Philadelphia provided me with a three-dimensional education about the dawning days of the United States of America. The places where history happened were not just pictures in books; they were real places, just a bus ride from our home.

Today, the U.S. Park Service administers most of these historic sites. School kids can no longer climb up onto Jefferson's chair, and a lot of the original artifacts have been taken away for safekeeping, with reproductions put in their place for the sake of the thousands of tourists who visit Independence Mall each day. The Liberty Bell no longer sits on an old wooden mount at the base of the tower staircase at the rear of Independence Hall. It is displayed a few hundred yards away, in its modern steel and glass-enclosed building. As a kid, I rubbed the smooth edges of the bell and traced the famous crack with my fingers. You can't do that anymore. In 2001, some nut job took a hammer to it, forcing the Park Service to increase security. The bell's new home is designed to help ensure that some lunatic would not deface this iconic symbol of liberty.

As a result of my early exposure to American history, I took an above-average interest in the Country's founding documents, particularly the Constitution. Like many Americans, I thought the Constitution consisted of multiple thick volumes, like the Encyclopedia Brittanica. But, in grade six, our handed out little palm-sized red, white, and blue booklets on the first day of class.

"This children, is the Constitution of The United States of America," Sister Mary Arthur said with solemnity. "It is the only document we will study this year."

Much to my amazement, the Constitution, with all the Amendments, fit into my shirt pocket. I spent middle school immersed in Constitutional history. It was great. Even though we all lived just a short bus or train ride away, most of the people in my neighborhood had never seen Independence Hall, let alone touched the Liberty Bell. I became a Junior Constitutional Scholar. Everyone, including Sister Mary Arthur, was sure I was destined for Law School. That wasn't in the cards. My short attention span and addictive tendencies put my life on a much different course. However, I am certain that even as a schoolboy, I understood the meaning and intent of The Constitution to a much greater degree than Donald J. Trump, the 45th and current President of the United States of America. This is why it pisses me off to no end to see him wipe his ass with it.

I don't think Trump is ignorant to the Constitutional Order; I think he just doesn't give a damn about the Law. He's been getting away with bending and breaking laws his entire life; so why change now?

One of the most grating things Trump does is refer to top-ranking military officers as "My Generals." This is the kind of talk espoused by despots and dictators. Either he doesn't know, or doesn't care that the military, from the lowest enlisted ranks to the highest brass, take an oath to the Constitution, not a particular President. He does the same thing with Law Enforcement Officers. He surrounds himself with hay-seed Sheriffs and small-town chiefs-of-police for photo ops and talks tough about how, "his police" are cleaning up America, making it great again. It's just dog-whistle-code for engaging in police brutality (with his blessing) towards brown and black people. Recently, surrounded by a motorcycle gang called "Bikers for Trump" and responding to questions about his political opposition on the left, Trump, in his familiarly painful word salad form, said: "You know, the left plays a tougher game, it's very funny, I actually think that the people on the right are tougher, but they don't play it tougher. Okay? I can tell you, I have the support of the police, the support of the military, the support of the bikers. I have the tough people, but they don't play it tough - until they go to a certain point, and then it would be very bad, very bad."

It doesn't take a stable genius to read between the lines and see that the sitting President of The United States is threatening violence towards those who would like to see him defeated at the polls.

Do I think there will be violence leading up to the 2020 presidential election? Yes, I do. Yes, on a scale that is unimaginable by most people who think that America is still the civilized "bright city on the hill." What will it look like? It will manifest as loosely organized groups of MAGA hooligans interrupting political rallies of Trump's Democratic opponents. At first, it will be threats and chest-bumping, neck-vein-popping, in-your-face, heated arguments. Then punches will fly. Then sticks and bats. Then chains and knives. Then BOOM! Gunfire splits the air and bodies will fall, horrific shrieking and blood-curdling screams will echo off buildings, and when the dust settles, we will be looking at inconceivable third-world-level political violence on the streets of America.

The white nationalists and fundamental Christians are systemically demonizing the Democratic Party and the left-leaning corporate media, (with the notable exception of Fox News). Right-wing provocateurs are dehumanizing them to the point of drawing figurative targets on their backs. Trump's political critics, including elected Members of Congress, are regularly receiving credible death threats. Referring to the free press as "the enemy of the people,"

Trump's volatile rhetoric has already resulted in intense violence at his "I Love Me" rallies. And don't forget the pipe bombs that a Trumpian devotee mailed to media personalities and liberal politicians. Trump's ignorant, flammable verbosity amplifies the American political and cultural differences to something akin to a domestic civil war. It is what the right-wingers want, and they have the weapons and the will to ignite the fuse in Trump's name.

Trump will find some way to separate himself from the carnage. He'll probably be golfing at one of his clubs when the shit-hits-the-fan. He isn't the type of guy to jump up on a tank like Boris Yeltsin did at the Soviet Parliament in 1991 when he ordered his loyal military units to open fire on the Supreme Soviet building with the legislators inside in an effort to save democracy. The politicians who opposed Yeltsin and led his impeachment were arrested by the military, ironically marking the event as the actual day that the fledgling Soviet democracy died. No, Donald Trump is the type of drunk with power guy that Yeltsin became a few years later, right before he was finally removed by the Soviet Parliament. So, there is a modern-day precedent for Trump to emulate.

If only little Donald had a chance to sit in Jefferson's chair or spend an entire school year with Sister Mary studying the U.S. Constitution, things might have turned out differently for him, and for America.

President for Life

I don't claim to be any more patriotic than the next person. And, of course, because I have left Trump's America and headed to Canada, many of you may read this and call me a traitor. After all, wouldn't a true patriot stay and fight for his country? Wouldn't a true patriot try to work from inside the system to change it? Perhaps.

My experience and sense of history tell me that the America I once knew is no more. I can smell despotism in the air. Oh yes, there are some promising signs like the election of new Democrats including a record number of women, in the last congressional election. Bright lights like New York's Alexandria Ocasio-Cortez and Ilhan Omar of Minnesota have hit the ground running and are giving the right-wing fits. But I think it is too little, too late. Their collective passion, integrity, and intellect are no match for a system of government that is rotten to its core. The amoral, greedy Establishment will permit them to voice opposition, but they will never be allowed anywhere near the actual levers of power. The status quo is serving the wealthy and powerful just as it is, and there are serious risks involved in upsetting the oligarchy. I fear for the safety of some of these newly-elected idealists.

As a young boy, I was a Cub Scout. It was a very odd thing for an inner-city kid like me to belong to an organization that went on overnight camping trips and taught wilderness skills. I had never been in a pure, natural environment. I was born and raised surrounded by the suffocating factories and mills of North Philadelphia. The narrow stream that ran a few blocks from our house was so dark, smelly and polluted that we were warned not to wade in it for fear of contracting diseases. It was nothing more than an open sewer. So, when on a July 4th weekend, I had the chance to get on a bus full of Cub Scouts and take a trip to a country lake, I was both excited and fearful. The main point of the trip was to earn our swim badges, but I couldn't swim and didn't want to drown. I didn't want to expose my weakness to the other kids, all of whom I was certain were just shy of Olympic-level swimmers. It was on this trip that I met my first politician.

A sitting Congressman's family owned the lakeside camp in the Pennsylvania Poconos. He was, of course, a Democrat. (LBJ was in the White House, and the country was still healing from the JFK assassination.) The

Congressman met our buses and manned the BBQ grill for our first day's lunch of hot dogs and cheeseburgers. He was a tall, toothy guy who seemed friendly. As it turned out, he was a competitive swimmer in his university days.

I was terrified of water deeper than my waist, so I was in for a rough time. It was during the first evening's splash around that I learned I was not the only boy who wasn't exactly a fish. It soon became apparent that a few of us from the city had only ever cooled ourselves under street corner fire hydrants. One of the weirdest sensations for me was feeling the aquatic plants touch my body and the lake bottom's sand squish between my toes. I was a concrete and asphalt creature, and all this wet nature was way too exotic for my comfort. But, driven by a desire not to be embarrassed, I tried really hard to swim. I watched the other boys and imitated them. I was very good for my age at most team sports like football, basketball, and baseball, but the inability to get this swimming stuff frustrated me.

Soon, the adults began breaking us up according to our proficiency in the water. I was sent over to the small group of non-swimmers. I thought we would be loaded up on the bus and shipped back to Philly, too inept to master a simple human skill as swimming. But we weren't banished from the lake, we were designated the "beginner class," and the

Congressman himself would be our swim coach. I thought he'd be more interested in the advanced kids, teaching them all the speed swimming secrets he learned as a competitor, but no, he hung out with us scrubs. The Congressman's trick was to instill confidence in us as young men, making us believe in ourselves. He showed us we could learn to swim by reinforcing our small achievements, like floating or doggie paddling for ten feet until we could all move on, supporting each other as a group. Soon, the boys who picked up basic swimming easily were helping the boys who were still struggling. By Sunday afternoon, every one of our remedial group could tread water and swim for fifty yards in the open water of the lake. We all earned our merit badges!

Because we were Cub Scouts, we ended our 4th of July weekend with a flag ceremony, campfire, and unpretentious fireworks. We marched around the lake, raised the flag and saluted it, and sang songs like "God Bless America." I was one of the boys chosen to lower Old Glory and solemnly fold it into the tri-corner field of blue with white stars. This may have been the most patriotic moment of my entire life.

It was all downhill from there.

As a Cub Scout, I developed an unrealistic perception of what a Member of Congressman was like. After all, a congressman taught me to swim, and seemed like a great guy! They must all be great guys who helped kids and cooked 4th of July hot dogs.

In the course of my idealistic life, I've had a chance to interact with a few Members of Congress. I met Joe Biden at a Delaware music festival when he was in his first Senate term. I was working the event as a stagehand, while Joe was glad-handing and cooking burgers on a grill. It was July 4th weekend, and he was running for reelection. This grilling must be a thing. He slipped backstage a few times to grab an icy beer from the crew's cooler and seemed like a nice, regular guy. I haven't seen anything of Joe Biden in the decades since that changes my mind. Now I wish he was not running to be the Democratic nominee for the presidency in 2020. I think he could be far more influential as the Democrat's elder statesman as they try to prevent Trump from burning America to the ground.

I've volunteered in political campaigns and met the candidates a few times. As a temporarily misguided Republican, I volunteered on Joe Scarborough's behalf. This amounted to standing on Pensacola street corners waving signs and helping the Republican Executive Committee organize some pub nights to raise money. Joe was a young lawyer and a genuinely nice man. I don't think he expected to win, but he did come out to the fundraisers and play some mean Bruce Springsteen covers with his band. Joe had the good sense to term-limit himself and move into broadcasting, and both of us ran screaming the Republican party

Much later in life, I found myself living in the Black Hills of South Dakota. I was working at the V.A. hospital when Senator Tom Daschle came for a visit. I was impressed with him and signed up as a local volunteer. The volunteers from the V.A. nurse's union, (of which I was a member) helped arrange a town hall forum by Daschle at the local American Legion. Maybe because I had previous experience as a stagehand, and owned a small P.A. system, I was chosen to provide the sound for the event. Senator Daschle arrived early and struck up a conversation with us at the side of the stage. As a fellow U.S. history buff, we struck up a conversation about the Founding Fathers and the rooms at Independence Hall that I visited as a child. Later that evening, he wove into his speech the story of Ben Franklin and the rising sun carved into George Washington's chair. I really liked him for that, but, as has too often been the case, the politicians I support, don't win. Daschle was upset by a new rising star of the GOP, John

Thune, who I believe the Republicans are grooming for the White House.

But, they may never get a chance if Trump has his way.

Many people believe as I do, that Donald Trump intends to remain, President, no matter the outcome of the next election. People like intelligence expert Malcolm Nance, who reminds us that Trump telegraphs his intentions all the time. When Trump praises dictators and strongmen across the globe, it isn't out of the goodness of his heart. He wishes he could rule by declaration, and his "reality show" executive order ceremonies are intended to soften up the American people into accepting his "decrees" as business as usual. Trump regards Chinese leader Xi Jinping as a role model.

"He's now president for life," Trump crowed. "President for life. No, he's great. And look, he was able to do that. I think it's great. Maybe we'll have to give that a shot someday." It doesn't take intelligence experts or psychologists to read between the lines and recognize that he wants to "give that a shot someday." He's telling us precisely what he intends to do. Donald Trump's attitude towards one of modern history's most evil and despotic rulers, Kim Jong Un, should be even more disturbing.

"I was really being tough and so was he," Trump said of the North Korean Boy-Emperor. "And we would go back and forth. And then we fell in love. No, really. He wrote me beautiful letters. They were great letters. And then we fell in love," he continued.

Holy shit! This is the President of the United States speaking of a man who has committed genocide against his own people by starving them, has brutally murdered his political opposition, including members of his own family, and has kept his country in a perpetual medieval darkness, lest his subjects rise up and challenge his power. And, so far, Trump has achieved nothing towards denuclearizing Kim. I'll also point out here that our president has sided with Kim Jong Un over the torture and eventual death of young American tourist Otto Warmbier. This is breathtaking. That an American President would praise a deranged dictator who arrests and tortures an American citizen for committing immature college high jinks, is monstrous. That he would believe that dictator over the counsel of the United States intelligence community is nothing less than appalling.

There are countless examples of Trump cow-towing to another dictator, Russia's Vladimir Putin. Whether he is aware of it or not, President Donald Trump is an asset of Russian Intelligence.

For my entire stint on active duty with the United States Navy and well into my Reserve time with the Army, the military units in which I served trained for a single scenario: a ground war against the Soviets in Europe. I have medals in the closet reminding me of that. So, it is particularly disheartening to watch the video of Trump in Helsinki, publicly siding with Putin, ignoring the advice of American Defense and Intelligence institutions. This, my sleepy, apathetic friends, may be the most dangerous thing Trump does in his first term: emboldening Putin to launch military aggression into some of the former Soviet states. He has already invaded Ukraine, via Crimea (with political and public relations cover from some of Trump's closest cronies), and Putin has his heart set on Estonia and other Eastern European prizes. Trump's failure to support the NATO Alliance is no fluke. Without NATO, people in Paris and Brussels are going to have to learn to speak Russian. And, like a New Jersey mob boss, Trump is trying to extort more money from America's closest allies, as if he's running some kind of NATO protection racket.

Trump has met privately with Putin, with no other American aides, advisers, or press in the room. There is even a case where Trump demanded that the interpreter give him their notes and swear an oath never to reveal what was discussed at the meeting. This behavior is not normal, people.

I believe that Trump is a dictator-in-waiting. He and his closest cronies (including Putin) are laying the groundwork for just such a scenario, and all the Alexandria Ocasio-Cortez's in the world won't stop him.

Nothing in my American life indicated that I would see such a possibility. As a flag-saluting young Cub Scout, or as a Navy SeaBee Petty Officer, I never once thought that the President of the United States was working against the best interests of the American people.

Until now.

MAGA Battalions

So, how is this nightmare scenario going to play out?

If you've been paying attention, Donald Trump has been hinting at how he intends to retain power indefinitely. As early as the first debates against Hillary Clinton, he began to plant the seed that the 2016 election may not be honest and fair. He repeatedly said it was rigged.

Of course, at the time, Trump was so far behind in the polls that most educated predictions of the outcome had Hillary winning by a significant margin. That's how I thought it would turn out too. But, it wasn't lost on me when Trump started to sow some doubt on the legitimacy of a Clinton win. My ears also perked up when he made the now-infamous call out to Russia. This is exactly what he said, from the transcripts of CNN:

TRUMP: "Why do I have to get involved with Putin? I have nothing to do with Putin. I've never spoken to him. I don't know anything about him other than he will respect me. He doesn't respect our President. And if it is Russia --

which it's probably not, nobody knows who it is -- but if it is Russia, it's really bad for a different reason, because it shows how little respect they have for our country, when they would hack into a major party and get everything. But it would be interesting to see -- I will tell you this -- Russia, if you're listening, I hope you're able to find the 30,000 emails that are missing. I think you will probably be rewarded mightily by our press. Let's see if that happens. That'll be next."

I think Comrade Vladimir was listening. In light of the events related to Russia and particularly Putin over the past two years, this is almost comically ironic, if it wasn't so troubling at the same time.

If you spend any time perusing the right-wing, white-supremacists conspiracy theory web forums, the plan is plain to see. Trump's cultists intend to disrupt the 2020 elections, with violence if necessary, to ensure their Messiah is re-elected. They will do it via physical intimidation, dirty tricks, and in places where they have control over the vote count, criminal electoral fraud. Don't be surprised to see Bikers for Trump blocking access to polling places in heavily liberal districts, minority areas, and universities. And in those counties across America where the Supervisor of Elections is a Trump loyalist, they will find ways to alter the vote totals to favor Trump. Remember the quote that is widely attributed to Russian dictator Joseph Stalin: "Those who cast the votes decide nothing; those who count the votes decide everything."

Russia again. My wife is convinced that the Russians already know the outcome of the 2020 election because they have spent years learning how to hack into American voting systems. Jill cites the 2006 documentary film, "Hacking Democracy," as a how-to primer for the Russians, or perhaps a "how they did it" warning for Americans. The film is about citizen-journalists investigating irregularities within American voting systems that were used in Florida during the 2000 and 2004 elections. They examine the machines made by Diebold Election Systems, uncovering faults and backdoors in the computer software. The Emmy nominated HBO movie ends with an on-camera hacking of the Diebold voting system used in Leon County, Florida. (The state capital, Tallahassee). This is the very same election hardware and software that is still used in many states across America. Don't be fooled. Diebold changed its name to Dominion Voting Systems, then to Premier Elections Solutions, but it is still the Dayton, Ohio based company that it was in 2004.

Russia has had more than a decade to study, test, and exploit the machine's vulnerabilities, and the Diebold systems are not the only ones that are open to exploitation. Technology has come a long way, and state-sponsored hacking and psychological operations are going to play a vital role in the next election.

If we Americans make it that far.

I know it seems almost impossible, but I am predicting that if Trump is impeached, or his re-election is seriously threatened, his white followers will take to the streets, and there will be riots unlike anything ever seen in America. I know that the pundits of DC and New York aren't going to tell you this, but I've got my ear to the ground on the frontlines of the MAGA battalions. I speak with them, watch their online chats and forums, and believe them when they say they are prepping for the next Civil War. Some of the people I know are aching for a chance to kill some of the "Snowflake Libs." Yes, I mean murder. There are deep psy-ops in place. First, demonize the Liberals as inhuman. Call them baby-killers who want to abort live children in the delivery room and sell their body parts., Call them all perverts, gays and transvestites, and label anyone with whom they don't agree as pedophiles and devil worshippers. It is a lot easier to draw a bead on a person you hate, a human you only see as a menace to orderly white society. It is okay to shoot your local baby-killing Satanists if you're doing the Lord's work.

And then there are the brown, black and Islamic people. They are easier to spot as targets. The Trump brigades see no harm in killing them because, to the MAGA crowd, they are subhuman invaders. This has been the genocidal script for centuries. Remember the "Injun' Hordes" who were raping and killing the white settlers in the Wild West? Yep, make it easier to exterminate them, male, female, and babies, by describing them as uncivilized savages. Remember the "Japs" in the Second World War? Yep, put all of the sneaky bastards you couldn't kill into internment camps right here in the U.S.A. and Canada. (Just ask George Takei about this.)

On active duty during Operation Desert Storm in 1991, we troops were brainwashed into dehumanizing the Iraqi people. Our leaders would show us videos and tell stories of atrocities, real and imagined, committed by these "Sand Niggers, Haji's and Camel Fuckers." Daddy Bush's administration put forth lies about Saddam ordering the deaths of babies in incubators. And, later, in GW's administration, the great "weapons of mass destruction" deception was effectively perpetrated.

The MAGA warriors are itching for a fight. When Trump surrounds himself with ICE agents or bikers in cuts and leathers, he's sending signals. The paid opinion pundits on MSNBC call it dog-whistling, meaning only Trump's hardcore followers can hear his calls to action. ICE is his equivalent to Hitler's NAZI Gestapo. (Okay, I made the inevitable comparison.) Bikers for Trump are just like Venezuelan President Nicolás Maduro's, "Colectivos."— The South American strongman's lawless but loyal paramilitary. If you want to see a sneak peek at what America will look like during the coming upheaval, Venezuela is a good example of societal chaos brought on by a rigged election, and an illegally appointed President. Sound familiar? Added to the South American political mess are weeks-long power outages, hyperinflation, and empty grocery store shelves. I'd give the U.S.A. about ten days of electoral chaos before a similar scenario plays out in the bigger cities.

Trump's middle-aged, disillusioned white male loyalists are so desperately lost in the 21st-century, they are easy for the right-wing to radicalize. They believe that brown people and immigrants have co-opted the way of life they once enjoyed. It won't take much to goad them to commit violence. An unhappy, emasculated, underemployed 55-

year-old man with a dozen firearms and a basement full of ammo will eagerly become a foot soldier in this new American culture war. Inspired by the digital echo chamber of Internet forums, right-wing radio, and Fox News, he thinks he is a patriot, called to cleanse America. He lives in a bubble of uncertainty, with no social safety net, no financial security, no one except his fellow toxic male white patriots to validate his cause. That quiet neighbor down the road that you wave to as he rides his John Deere mower might just be squeezing the trigger soon on your daughter's Mexican-American boyfriend. After all, he's just cleaning up the neighborhood and making America great again.

I am convinced that Donald Trump expects his bikers, klansmen, dirty cops, and mercenaries to rally around him when the inevitable time comes for him to leave office. One of my greatest fears is that, like many dictators before him, he has made side deals with certain high ranking military leaders to lend their troops to his cause, citing a coup by the left. Trump is already introducing this nebulous idea of a coup, labeling some FBI counter intelligence investigations from early in his presidency as illegal coup attempts. If this day ever comes, and Trump attempts to maintain power and control by violence and military threats, it is the end of the noble experiment known as the United States of America.

20/20 Vision

At the direction of Trump's new Attorney General William Barr, the long-awaited Mueller Report was wrapped up and turned over. In a superhuman act of speed-reading and redaction, Barr and others at the Justice Department studied and interpreted the 400-page document in under two days. Barr sent letters to the Leaders of the relevant committees on Capitol Hill stating that:

"After reviewing the Special Counsel's final report on these issues; consulting with Department officials, including the Office of Legal Counsel; and applying the principles of federal prosecution that guide our charging decisions, Deputy Attorney General Rod Rosenstein and I have concluded that the evidence developed during the Special Counsel's investigation is not sufficient to establish that the President committed an obstruction of justice offense."

That's when the first cranial detonation was heard 'round the world. In William Barr's opinion, based on the investigation Mr. Mueller conducted over the course of two years, President Trump DID NOT collude or conspire with the Russians to influence the 2016 election. Simply put into Trump Twitter Speak: NO-COLLUSION, TOTALLY EXONERATED, MAGA!

This, as it has been recently revealed, is at odds with Mueller's actual findings. Robert Mueller made clear that he did not determine that Trump hadn't obstructed justice, and said that, "if we had had confidence the president clearly did not commit a crime we would have said so."

The issue of obstruction was left up to chief referee Barr and head linesman Rod Rosenstein to make the call. Despite the report's findings, they called it: No harm, no foul, no whistle on the play: no penalty flag thrown, and no red cards. Although limping a bit, Trump is still on the field calling the plays.

How many "It's Mueller Time" t-shirts do you think will sell on Amazon now? From New York to Los Angeles, D.C. to Chicago, Democrats, Liberals, Progressives, and Socialists are licking their organic, sea-salt-filled wounds. The anguish and gnashing of teeth on the left is palpable. Heads are exploding, splatting against the walls in the newsrooms of CNN, MSNBC, The New York Times and Washington Post. Perhaps they placed an overabundance of faith in the Mueller Report. Liberal pundits characterized the Special Counsel as a white hat-wearing Sheriff who was going to clean out the O.K. Corral of the outlaw the Trump Gang. This whole "waiting on a Messiah" mentality is bullshit, and bullshit stinks just as awful on the left as the right. There is no wizard surfing in on a rainbow to save America.

The people who can save America are getting up on Monday morning, going to work, and by Friday evening will be so numb, so sick of the politics of discord, that all they want to do is drink a few beers, maybe smoke some weed, watch some Netflix and get the kids to soccer practice on Saturday morning. Somewhere during the weekend, they hope to squeeze in some lovemaking with their partner, so that they can feel human again. Then, the Monday morning alarm will scream, reminding them they are just tax-paying-cogs, useless eaters in the great inequitable scheme to make America great again for their political and corporate masters.

The working classes of America are the best hope for the long term viability of what passes for Democracy in the 21st century. Yes. We are so fucked.

I have said all along that Donald Trump will survive everything the Dems throw at him. He just survived their biggest conventional weapon - The Mueller Investigation.

Now, the question is: will the Democrats choose the nuclear option and begin impeachment proceedings? Who knows? Impeachment would undoubtedly divide the country beyond recognition. But, there is zero chance that a majority Republican Senate will convict Trump, so he doesn't even need to retreat to the political fallout shelter. His base loves this. The 35% or so that make up his most fervent devotees look at the Mueller Report as a great victory for their Savior. The MAGA Brigades are learning the meaning of a new vocabulary word: exonerated. Trump and his minions live in a zero-sum world of winners and losers. Right now, they feel like big winners. And the Resistance, the Never Trumpers? They look pretty impotent. Losers with a capital "L."

I don't know if Attorney General Barr was put into place for just this moment or not, but, he is a hand-selected Trump appointee. And, if you want to play out the partisan political conspiracy, remember that Barr, Rosenstein, and Mueller are life-long Republicans. (As were former FBI Directors Comey, and McCabe). Whether they can stomach him or not, Donald Trump is the Republican President of the United States. And, don't forget they are mostly rich white guys, and rich white guys seem to cover for each other. Look at Brett Kavanaugh. He has a fresh new wardrobe filled with crisply-starched black judge's robes. Against all evidence that he had a questionable past, and really, really liked beer to the point where he blacked out, a bunch of rich white guys, led by Donald Trump, put Kavanaugh on the Supreme Court. I'm sure they remind him of this frequently, just in case they need to call in a favor someday. It can even be argued that twice-convicted Trump Campaign Chairman Paul Manafort was a recent recipient of the rich, white-guy privilege. Although Robert Mueller's prosecutorial team recommended up to twenty-four years in prison for his numerous crimes, committed over a span of several decades, rich, white-guy Manafort only got 7 1/2 years. I used to work in state prisons. There are brown people sitting in those places doing twenty years for selling some weed in the parking lot of a Walmart. Due to the mandatory minimum sentences adopted in the 80s' and 90s', men and women are doing hard time for selling a naturally occurring plant that is now legal in many U.S. states and all across Canada. Ironic isn't it? The folks busted for selling dope at the street-level are definitely not in the rich, white-guy club. It is a good bet that Mar-a-Lago is the new rich, white-guy command post. It is also a good bet that some Mar-a-Lago members have partaken in the illegal drug trade, either as users, buyers, or sellers. But, they won't do a minute behind bars because they are rich white-guys who pay two hundred-thousand dollars a year for access to Donald Trump through membership at his exclusive resort and golf club. This is a good place to quote Nobel Laureate, Robert Zimmerman:

"Now all the criminals in their coats and their ties
Are free to drink martinis and watch the sun rise…"
- Bob Dylan, *Hurricane*

We need to stop expecting people with no sense of decency, or respect for ethics, and no idea of right and wrong, to do the right thing. They don't live by the same rules as the rest of us, yet we keep electing them to high office and granting them positions of power.

I am not a rich, white guy. I have however been on the receiving end of white male privilege. Any middle-aged white man in America knows that we are given the benefit of the doubt in society. A few years ago, I was stopped at a sobriety checkpoint and didn't have my driver's license on me. It was just a brain fart, where I changed clothes before I went out and left my wallet in my other pants. I also had a loaded pistol in the center console of my vehicle. When I rolled into the brightly-lit checkpoint, I lowered my window and stopped next to the two officers in charge. They shined powerful flashlights in my eyes, and almost blinded, I answered their questions.

"Where you going, sir?"

"I just ran into town to check my post office box. I'm heading home now," I said.

"Where do you live?" the officer asked.

"Right down the highway here, just before you turn onto the state road."

"Have you had any alcohol to drink today, sir?" the officer asked.

"No, sir, I haven't had anything to drink in over a decade," I said. I wanted him to catch the code for, "I'm sober."

"Whose car is this?", the cop asked.

"Mine. My wife and I own it," I said.

"Can I see the registration, please?", one of the officers said.

I reached over to the console.

"Officer, I have a firearm in the console where I keep the registration. What do you want me to do?"

"Keep your hands where we can see them, slowly open the door, and when you come out of the vehicle put your hands on the hood of the car," he instructed.

"Yes sir, no problem."

"Slow-ly," they reminded me.

I did as told. I stood at the front left quarter panel with my hands on the warm, dusty hood. One of the cops went around and opened the passenger side door, leaned in, popped open the console and with his big Maglite, shined it inside. He also looked under the seats and in the rear of the car. To my surprise, he did not touch my gun. He carefully picked up the little clear plastic document holder that had the car registration inside. I also kept my concealed weapon permit in there, but he didn't take it out.

Here's where my perceived white privilege played a part. After radioing in my car registration info, the officer put the card back into the console and closed the passenger door. He looked over at me and said, "Okay, you are free to go, sir." They never asked my name. They never asked for my driver's license. They saw I had a loaded, concealed firearm in the car. I was allowed to continue on home with no hassle.

They were all white males, some about my age, and like me, a few of them had shaved heads and visible tattoos. It is a good bet that if I were a black man, my experience would have been remarkably different, maybe even fatal.

It says a lot about a country, when a law-abiding citizen avoids contact with law enforcement, lest they have a misunderstanding that costs them their life. Most of the American black guys I know want nothing to do with the police. And, these are not gang bangers or outlaws. These are regular people, some of them military veterans, who consciously avoid the police. Their experience with the cops has been influenced by a lifetime of police abuse and brutality. If not experienced first hand, they know someone who has suffered on the business end of a baton, taser, chokehold or steel-toed boot.

As long as Donald Trump sets the racist tone in Washington, things will not get better. And, as far as I can tell, there will be at least two more years of the Trump administration calling the shots.

The perceived exoneration of Donald Trump and his campaign in the Russian interference investigation also means at least two more years of chaos in Washington. Trump and his supporters seem very cocky now that the William Barr interpretation of the Mueller findings has cleared the President. But, that's not the whole story. The entire story resides in the complete, unredacted Mueller investigation report, which will probably never see the light of day. The Democratic House can demand to see it until they are blue in the face, but Barr and Trump have no legal obligation to turn it over. And they won't, even if the Court orders them to give it up.

Rachel Maddow and some of the regular progressive savants over on MSNBC have been more than a bit somber of late. In a depressive daze, they seemed shocked to their cores. A few days after William Barr's summary, Ms. Maddow laid out a neat, bullet-pointed list of questions that should be asked by the Democratic House. In what reality are the Liberals living? The reality is that no one at the Justice Department or Executive Branch gives a rat's ass what Maddow, the liberal Dems or Congress want. They are using the "No Collusion" illusion to pivot right into the 2020 presidential election. As hard as it is to admit, Trump has gained steam as a result of the two year Mueller investigation.

Trump-supporting stooges who regularly post on Internet discussion forums are absolutely ecstatic right now. Emboldened by their perceived win, they are calling for the heads of the Democrats who oppose their Dear Leader. The "Lock Her Up" chorus is morphing into "Lock Them Up," and the accusations that Obama, Comey, and Clinton are traitors who deserve nothing less than to be strung up, is a common theme. If you want to take the temperature of the far, far right, don't watch Fox News, go log on to GodlikeProductions.com or peruse /r/TheDonald subReddit online. Fox News is for your retired grandparents. Godlike and The Donald are where the foot soldiers hang out. If you want to lose faith in the sanity of the American electorate, watch a few minutes of the Patriot's Soapbox on YouTube. This is where the most delusional "QAnon" disciples converse, convinced that there is a well-organized conspiracy to bring down Donald Trump led by Barack Obama, the Clintons, and other members of the elite "Deep State." And, then there are the homes of the political sociopaths among us, and I don't mean the Republican National Committee. The most dangerous white supremacists and toxic right-wing males gather at loosely moderated chat and image forums like Storm Front, 4Chan and more lately, 8Chan. Go to these websites once, and you will never complain about hate speech on Facebook or Twitter again. The "Chans" used to be the unmoderated discussion and loosey-goosey soft-porn playground of fifteen-year-olds. Now, they are the not-so-secret online clubs where "incels," and extremists communicate in subtle codewords about violence towards Liberals, women, and queers. It is the price of living in an open society I suppose, but when I check out these websites, I feel a sense of dread.

They are full of marginalized, depressed young men, encouraging each other to sociopathic, violent behavior. More than one mass shooter left fresh footprints on 4Chan and 8Chan. They will answer the call for violence when their Dear Leader asks them to take his fight out of their mom's basements and onto the streets.

My Canadian neighbors don't understand why the United States Attorney General claims that the Mueller investigation does not prove direct evidence of collusion between Trump and the Russians in the 2016 elections. To them, the fact that Micheal Cohen, Paul Manafort and Mike Flynn, as well as several others, have already been convicted of campaign crimes surely implicates Trump, doesn't it? As the resident American in this small community, I get asked questions for which I have no simple answers. At the risk of sounding too much like Rodney King—a man who was beaten within an inch of his life by a raving mob of LAPD cops—many well-meaning Canadians ask, "Why can't you Americans just get along?" That is the $64,000 question. Why do Americans cling to their cultural differences and express them to the point of violence?

Canadians express a sense of "Canadian-ness." Even though they come from every corner of the planet, once they find themselves welcomed here, they embrace most things Canadian. Yes, they have many distinct political and cultural differences, but with four or five major political parties, and an entire province that speaks a different first language, Canadians still manage to maintain civility. They respect opposing viewpoints. They don't threaten to lock up the loyal opposition. They simply get along, even with those with whom they have disparate political views.

In my lifetime, I have never seen Americans so divided. The polarization will only get worse as the 2020 elections approach. The potential for chaos and politically motivated violence scares the shit out of me.

Divided We Fell

Okay, America, you asked for a Constitutional crisis, and there is one sitting right in front of you. Ever since his hand-picked Attorney General William Barr told Donald Trump that that Mueller report does not prove collusion between him and the Russians, the President has been on a raging Twitter tear. He's back to calling the free press the enemy of the people and threatening to close the border with Mexico completely. But, the most troubling behavior he has recently displayed is calling for the ousting of prominent Democratic Members of Congress—most prominently California Congressman Adam Schiff, Chairman of the House Intelligence Committee. Schiff's committee has the power to investigate and subpoena many of the main cast of characters in the Russian collusion matter, including Special Counsel Robert Mueller himself. It is no surprise that Trump immediately attacked Schiff, one of the people who has the power to hurt him the most. Encouraged by Trump, the Republican members of Schiff's committee have called for a vote on their steadfast

Chairman's ouster. It failed, with the votes cast along party lines.

In refusing to turn over the Mueller report, Trump and Barr have built a wall around the Administration and shut out Congress, the Press, and the People. By comparison, when Kenneth Starr investigated Bill Clinton, his findings were delivered to Congress on a Wednesday, and by Friday they were made available to the media and the public.

The bottom line is that the Executive Branch of the United States has gone rogue, completely defying the legitimate powers of oversight granted by the Constitution to the Representative Branch. This is going to get very ugly, very soon.

So, amid all this chaos, what does Trump do? He holds a rally! Emboldened by Barr's interpretation of the Mueller investigation, his followers turned to celebration. Of course, they haven't read the report. Nobody, outside of a few very privileged members of the DOJ have seen the un-redacted Mueller report. Yet, the Trumpsters are declaring victory simply based on their Dear Leader's interpretation of the results as a two-year "Witch Hunt." The new, incendiary chants are, "No Collusion," "Vindication," and "Completely Exonerated," although the last war cries may have sent many a Trumpster to crack open a dusty dictionary for the first time in years.

Congress seems unable to control the runaway Trump train. I think it careened off the tracks back when Homeland Security began separating families at the border, putting kids in cages, and shipping babies to the far corners of the country. But, the American public has a short memory, so the whole "Babies in Cages" uproar petered out fast. Trump forced the ouster of Kirstjen Nielsen, the cabinet member he conveniently blamed for the mess at the border. Problem solved. Once a respected Washington insider, all Ms. Nielsen will now be remembered for is snatching crying babies from their mother's arms.

Rumors suggest that Trump fired Nielsen for failing to follow his most atrocious orders. But, I don't shed a single tear for her. Like many former cabinet-level officials, she will land a big job at a university or think-tank, or maybe even a recurring guest-spot on Fox News. For good measure, Trump also fired the head of the United States Secret Service and purged a host of other vital deputies and assistants in the U.S. intelligence and security apparatus.

The dysfunctional Trump administration is now without a permanent:

Homeland Security Director

Secret Service Director

ICE Director

Secretary of Defense

Air Force Secretary

FEMA Director

Secretary of the Interior

UN Ambassador

White House Chief of Staff

Labor Secretary

- And dozens of ambassadorial and staff positions at the Department of State. Hell, he's even managed to influence the removal of diplomats of other nations, like the recent U.K. Ambassador to the United States.

For more than a year, I've been telling anyone who will listen that Trump and his cronies are systematically dismantling the Ship of State and selling it for scrap. In conspiratorial left-wing circles, the words "coup d 'état," and "dictatorship," are being thrown around by some very smart, informed people. When you step back and look at the results of the Donald Trump administration's firings, resignations, appointments and hires, it becomes clear that he is ousting anyone who questions him or challenges his unlawful orders. His appointment of "acting" secretaries and department heads is nothing more than an end-run around the Senate vetting process. Taken a step further, it also prevents his newly-minted appointees from establishing their own departmental fiefdoms. A duly nominated and Senate approved cabinet-level Secretary would bring in their personal trusted aides and assistants. (Ironically, that's how Kirstjen Nielsen landed her gig at Homeland Security. She was an aide to former White House Chief-of-Staff, General John Kelly.) But, without a permanent position in the Administration on offer, no ambitious, experienced Washington operator would jump into these shark-infested Trumpian waters. It would not be an excellent longterm career move. Drain the swamp, indeed. Drain it of anyone who has the experience and expertise to competently navigate the federal bureaucracy. Competence is a threat to Trump. He does not ask for proficiency in the people who surround him; he demands only one trait, loyalty. However, loyalty to Trump does not imply loyalty to Country. Observe the original cast of aides and advisors who have managed to hang on to their key positions: Kelley Ann Conway, whose job it is to get on TV and lie for Trump; Stephen Miller, who has Trump's ear and, it seems, is the guiding force behind the efforts to purify America via sadistic and quasi-legal immigration policies; Jared Kushner and Ivanka Trump, who, I'm not certain anyone can nail down their actual roles in the White House, but are proof-positive that nepotism is the gift that keeps on giving.

It hurts me to see my fellow Americans so driven apart, so at odds with one another over the politics of Trump. I can't believe they don't see how he and his mob of swindlers are pillaging the country and selling their dangerous ideology like shit sandwiches to hard-working people who seem happy to eat crap for these power-addicted madmen. Trump doesn't care one iota about the working man. They are nothing but annoying pimples on his big orange ass. He uses farmers, truck drivers and coal miners as props for his photo-ops. Swept into his false narrative, the workers believe he can relate to them. They naively believe this son-of-a-millionaire, born into inherited wealth and privilege, understands their knuckle-busting plight. They want a hero to raise them from their self-limiting mediocrity. They long for a caucasian champion who will rescue them from the brown invaders who are coming to turn their safe white neighborhoods into dangerous Spanish speaking barrios. Trump's supporters have been brainwashed into believing that caravans of rapists from three different Mexico's are coming for their jobs and to kidnap their daughters, causing them to endure a future of mocha-skinned grand-babies. It is inconceivable to me that these MAGA-hat-wearing, jingoistic men and women are the Baby Boomers who led the world in the 20th century. When did they become so fearful, ignorant, and bigoted?

In Your Name

I admit that I find myself missing the warm, early springs I enjoyed in North Florida. We have had so much cold snow in Ontario this winter that I have shifted into survival mode. Mother Nature has challenged me, testing whether I am genuinely committed to this "moving to Canada" thing. Ottawa, the nation's capital and largest nearby city, has broken snowfall records several times over this winter. I can endure colossal snowstorms in January, but by mid-April, there is an eight-foot mountain of residual snow piled in the corner of our condo parking lot.

So, in a chilly moment of weakness, hoping that making contact with warmer climes would lift my wintry spirits, I decided to call and check in with Doug.

"Hey Doug, how are things in Trumpistan?"

"Very funny, Robert. How are things in Commie Canada? Is Justine soy-boy still in charge?" he quipped.

For some reason, Canadian Prime Minister Justin Trudeau is depicted by the American right-wing as an effeminate weakling. The reality is that Trudeau is a remarkably fit and physically strong amateur boxer, a martial arts student, swimmer, scuba diver, and kayaker. Yet, the ill-informed MAGA Americans choose to portray him as a wussy. I guess their image of a strong and fit leader is a grossly overweight man in his 70s' with a fake orange tan and belly that gets in the way of his awful golf swing.

Trudeau and his Foreign Minister Chrystia Freeland have become stones in Trump's shoes as he tries to bully Canada into unfavorable trade deals. Hence, Trump shows disdain for them, and the nation of Canada in general, even to the ridiculous point of claiming Canada is a security risk to the United States. It is more likely that the younger, handsome, and intelligent Trudeau is a threat to Donald Trump's insecure masculinity.

After exchanging some pleasantries about life in general, Doug steered our phone conversation back to the familiar territory of American politics.

"Well, now that Trump has been exonerated, are you moving back?" he asked.

"No and no," I said, "He's not exonerated and I'm never moving back."

I realized this was the first time I expressed myself this way: "Never-moving-back." I still consider Doug to be a great friend. In spite of our philosophical differences and our dissimilar political leanings, we have always been fond of each other. During this phone call, it dawned on me that Canada was now my home, and I preferred to live among Canadians. My former home of Florida and the U.S., in general, was now the "other place." In a way, I believe my moving away hurt Doug's feelings. We had established a bond over a decade, and I missed this weird friendship. I assume he missed my company as well. Men sometimes express affection as taunting, or "yanking someone's chain," and I believe Doug is a master at this.

"So, Robert," he continued, "are you putting maple syrup on your bacon and drinking milk from a bag?"

The whole "milk in a bag" thing is unique to Ontario. It still looks strange to me, and maybe when it doesn't, that's the moment when I will be truly Canadian. As for maple syrup, there is nothing that it doesn't make taste better. Maple syrup is so integral to Canadian life that in the province of Quebec there is actually a warehouse containing the country's strategic maple syrup reserve. It is liquid gold around here. By sheer luck, and no accident, we moved to Canada's maple capital, a county overflowing with the syrupy brown goodness.

During our conversation, Doug admits he is getting tired of the constant barrage of right vs. left political theatre. Doug has been turning inward and hasn't been interacting very much with the extremist element of the local citizen's militia.

"Some of the guys want to go over to Texas and patrol the border. I'm not up for that shit, playing wanna-be Border Patrol," he said.

Doug is blessed with far more common sense than most of the men in the local militia.

"Geez Doug, someone's going to get hurt or arrested if they do that," I said.

"Well, let the dumb asses go. I'm all for protecting our place and helping each other when the shit hits, but I don't agree with rounding up migrants all the way over in Texas. Let the Texans take care of Texas," said Doug. "Shit, if we didn't have a few Mexicans around these parts here, the watermelons would rot in the fields all over this county."

Well, this is a little progress. Doug hasn't ever been mean, but he has expressed mild acrimony towards brown-skinned immigrants. Like a lot of people in Gilchrist County, he's okay with itinerant Mexican field workers picking the produce, but after the work is done, they had better move on up north following the seasonal harvests. I don't think he wants a family of Mexican migrants moving into the house that's for sale on the lot next to him. But, refusing to join the vigilantes on the border is undoubtedly smart. The rest of my call with Doug was mostly middle-aged male smart-assery and updates on the old home town. Overall, I'm not feeling very nostalgic, but checking in with Doug reminded me that, despite our differences, we found common respectable ground and developed a sincere friendship. Again, I scratch my head and wonder why others who disagree can't find a way to engage each other on common ground.

Even with the slight headway toward tolerance I sensed in Doug, I wrestle with the reasons why so many Americans are vehemently anti-immigrant. The apparent conundrum is that most Americans have either immigrated to these shores themselves or have a short timeline back to ancestors who did. Doesn't the MAGA crowd realize that Donald Trump's mother, Mary Anne MacLeod, was born in the Outer Hebrides of Scotland and immigrated to the United States in the 1930s'? She was welcomed as a naturalized citizen in 1942. Donald J. Trump, the 45th President of the United States, is the middle son of a humble immigrant mother. Trump's father Frederick, the noted real estate mogul and source of Donald's inherited wealth, is the son of Bavarian German immigrants. Donald Trump has five children from three different marriages. Four of his five kids were born to immigrant mothers: Don Jr., Ivanka, and Eric from his marriage to Czech-born Ivana Zelnickova, and his young son Barron with Slovenia native Melania Knavs, the current First Lady. (The immigration circumstances of Melania and her parents are a bit suspect, but I'll give her the benefit of the doubt because she has to endure being married to Donald.) You would think a guy with an immigrant mother and wives would be a little more sympathetic towards others who want to come to live in the Land of Opportunity.

So, what's the difference between Trump's immigrant family and those being illegally rounded up at the southern border by armed citizen militias and vigilante groups? If you guessed "skin tone" go to the head of the class. The Scottish and Bavarian ancestors on Trump's family tree are white Europeans; the migrants currently seeking asylum at the United States border are a little on the brown side. And, in Trump's own words, they come from "shit hole countries" like Guatemala, Honduras, and El Salvador. These immigrants are escaping war, violence, injustice, and oppression. Somehow, the Americans I once thought I knew, who would welcome them with the same open arms that greeted Mary Anne MacLeod, have turned hostile towards those seeking safety and asylum. Let me be clear. The immigrants showing up at U.S. border stations are legally seeking asylum. They are not sneaking across the border. They are following the rules. They are following established lawful procedures to enter the United States. These immigrants have done nothing wrong - they simply seek what many of our ancestors dreamed of: A better life and opportunities for their children. Just like the McClellans who preceded me. Just like the Trumps who very recently arrived in America. Just like my Canadian wife who, as a young woman, followed a career that landed her legally living and working in America.

Jill is a naturalized American citizen. Her immigration experience was expensive and riddled with red tape and bureaucracy. Not once was she forcibly separated from her family or tear-gassed. But she is a white, middle-class Canadian woman and her forebears are of English and Welsh origin, among the whitest of all white people who ever walked the earth.

Immigrants aren't the problem. The right-wing using immigration as a divisive issue is the problem. Trump and his sycophants have managed to turn a boring administrative procedure - immigration and naturalization -

into the leading wedge issue of his presidency. Why? Because it stirs up fear in the bellies of the bigots. With cries of "The Caravans are Coming," Trump and his underlings have ginned up the fear of immigrants to a feverish pitch. They keep singing the same tired refrain: They are rapists, drug dealers, and MS-13 gang-bangers. They are not sending their "best people."

They are coming to steal your jobs!

Let me clue you in on a little secret: If you are lucky enough to have a good job, almost everyone who works below and beside you is gunning for it. No matter what skin color they are, or which way of life they practice, almost every intern and new graduate who shows up at the HR department to be interviewed wants to push you out of your cushy gig. They would happily steal your job and not think twice about how it affects you. Would you support tear-gassing them or throwing their kids into cages because they want your position? Would you arrest them and have them put into a detention camp if they walked into your bosses' office and claimed to be better suited for your job than you are?

I bet you wouldn't.

Then tell me, my American brothers and sisters, why do you allow an out of control federal agency with badges and guns to do the very same thing, in your name, at your country's borders? To protect your job, and prevent others from seeking the same opportunities you have enjoyed, in your name they are using force against defenseless people who walked to the border from Central America. In your name, to protect your career, they are snatching crying babies from the arms of loving parents. Oh, right, they are murderous hordes of little brown people from the shit hole countries invading in massive caravans that only exist in Donald Trump's mind.

Tell me, my American friends, why do you fear that MS-13 mobs are streaming across your borders? Don't you know that "Mara Salvatrucha," the full name of MS-13, is an international criminal gang that originated in California? That's right here in the good ol' United States of America. MS-13 came into existence because families of Salvadoran immigrants organized to protect themselves from anti-immigrant violence in the Los Angeles area. I used to work in prisons, up close and personal with some inmates who are MS-13 members. They are serious people and unquestionably a criminal enterprise. But, MS-13 is not sneaking across the border, hidden among breastfeeding women and runny-nosed children. They make a lot of dirty money with their illegal activities and use that cash to buy expensive suits and fly first-class from Central America into Boston, L.A., and Philadelphia. They aren't trudging through the Mexican desert in flip flops. MS-13 has begun to encourage their younger members to forego the iconic, menacing face tattoos, so they may better fit in with mainstream American society. I guess you could call it a tiny first step towards assimilation.

And why, my American friends is it okay for the President to embrace one type of gang - let's say biker gangs - and demonize another group like MS-13? Oh yeah, I forgot, most MS-13 members are brown people, and most of the bikers I see pictured with Trump are middle-aged white guys dressed like cosplay pirates. Trust me; the white bikers aren't boy scouts either.

And why, my American sisters do you fear a young Guatemalan mother with two children arriving at your border? Don't you know that woman is escaping abuse, violence, and oppression? She is seeking an education for her children. She wants a safe place to raise her family. She is seeking honest work so that she can provide, as a single mother, for her babies. Just like you. Why do you condone the Border Patrol tear-gassing her little daughter when they arrive at the fence seeking asylum and relief from the horrors of her life? In your name, they do this. Why do you approve of your president ordering those crying children to be wrested from their parent's arms, never to see their distraught family again? Yes, in your name.

And, why, my American Christian brothers and sisters do you not practice your faith as Jesus asked you? Why don't you give shelter to those who seek safety? Why don't you feed the hungry and the poor? Don't you know that most of the people from Mexico and Central America who show up at the border are also Christians? They were proselytized and converted by missionaries from your very own churches, yet here they are, standing right in front of you and you deny them. Don't take my word for it, listen to the words of your favorite persecuted brown guy - Jesus Christ, a Middle-Eastern native of Nazareth, in Matthew 25:

"Come, you that are blessed by my Father, inherit the kingdom prepared for you from the foundation of the world; for I was hungry and you gave me food, I was thirsty and you gave me something to drink, I was a stranger and you welcomed me, I was naked and you gave me clothing, I was sick and you took care of me, I was in prison and you visited me."

The larger question is: Why do you allow a paranoid, narcissistic sociopath like Donald Trump make these inhumane decisions for you?

In your name.

Get Your Passport

My Fellow Americans: Get your passport. If you already have one, make sure it is up-to-date. If you don't have one, go online and begin the application process. Now. Today. ASAP.

In January 2021, when the tanks are surrounding the White House to keep the angry populace at bay, you will wish you did. Don't forget; you heard it here first: Walls work both ways.

Tony Swartz, (the real "Art of the Deal" writer) knows Donald Trump better than almost anyone. He predicted Trump would do three things: He'd attack the free press; he'd compile an enemies list and begin getting revenge on those he thinks slighted him; and he'd declare martial law to solidify his power.

No matter the outcome of the next election, Donald John Trump intends to remain President-for-Life. And, considering the current state of the other so-called "co-equal" branches of the federal government, there is no indication they will forcibly oust him. He's not leaving, people.

The United States is about to become a tough place for a progressive, open-minded, educated person to thrive.

If you currently have the financial means to leave Trump's America, you may want to begin researching what countries to which you may like to move. If you have a marketable skill, especially a professional certification in engineering, medicine, or technology, you may want to start looking at which countries are seeking people like you.

Despite the generally misplaced claim made by many Americans that the United States is the best country in the world, it really is not. Look at any independent survey or university study ranking nations on personal freedom, healthcare, education, or quality of life, and you'll find America behind dozens of others. This hurts me - it is not a result I find acceptable. As a member of the Baby Boom generation, I also accept some responsibility for America's fall from grace. When we had the chance to put America on a better course, we were asleep at the switch. Maybe we are the self-absorbed, consumer-oriented, media junkie generation that our children accuse us of being. We replaced critical thinking with daily diatribes by Rush

Limbaugh, Sean Hannity, and Anderson Cooper. Many of us are certainly politically apathetic. Only a little over half of the eligible voters turned out for the last U.S. presidential election. We stopped paying attention to politics and replaced our civic engagement with tailgate parties, wine-o'clock, and binge-watching dramatic T.V. series on cable. (One exception: the HULU TV adaptation of esteemed Canadian author Margaret Atwood's "The Handmaid's Tale" sure seems to be the 2019 guidebook for certain authoritarian types in America.) Our generation lost interest in the arts and humanities, replacing them with trash T.V. and celebrity mediocrity. Is it any wonder that a famous reality television star now sits at the Resolute Desk in the oval office? I've often said that most Americans won't discover they have lost their country until NASCAR stops racing and "Keeping Up with the Kardashians" is not on the tube.

For some reason, some of my Boomer generation thought it would be a great idea to heavily medicate our children when they expressed original, non-conforming behaviors. I think parents will look back on this practice in horror. Force-feeding grade schoolers anti-psychotics and anti-depressants smacks of pharmacologic eugenics, implemented by state-licensed teachers and doctors. We have created a generation of the living dead, uncomfortable with, and unable to thrive in a society where it is crucial to possess the ability to socialize and process emotions. They resort to cutting themselves, so that they can feel alive. And, at the extreme level of their frustrations, they shoot up classrooms, churches, and mosques. Isn't it clear that the frequent violent attacks on these institutions are a statement about the failure of these same organizations to educate and provide a moral compass in the community?

We American Baby Boomers have a lot to account for.

I'm not claiming that Canada, my new home, is perfect. Far from it. Canadians are experiencing some of the same challenges as much of the Western world. There is a growing far-right nationalist movement in Canada, notably in the province of Alberta. Whether it was exported from America or home grown, the Canadian Alt-Right is gaining converts, especially among displaced oil field workers and other blue collar white people. These northern cousins of the KKK and Storm Front are also whinging about immigrants, mostly refugees fleeing war-torn Syria and Africa. The big difference here is that outside the shadowy world of the white supremacists, Joe Average Canadian welcomes immigration. Church and community groups, and at times, individual families, provide the resources to sponsor entire families, helping them to make a smoother transition to life in Canada. (My wife's parents sponsored a Vietnamese family, and every one of their grown children has earned an advanced university degree and is practicing a profession.) Just think about this for a moment - the Canadian Prime Minister, Justin Trudeau, has been known to meet arriving refugee families at airports, offering welcoming handshakes, hugs, and warm jackets to the newest Canadian families. Can you imagine Donald Trump doing this? As great of a photo op that it is, he'd never be seen hugging a Muslim man at the LaGuardia arrival lounge. The only time I've seen Trump offer a hug, it was a creepy half-hump of the American flag. I don't think Donnie's a big hugger. Or a hand-holder. Ask "Melanie."

The Canadian economy is also experiencing occasional bumps in the road. The housing ownership market in major cities like Vancouver and Toronto is beyond the means of most young people. They are living six to a house, subletting shared rooms for over $1000 per month. According to a 2019 CBC report, the average price of a single-family home or condo in Toronto was CAD 824,336. Many neighborhoods are well above a million dollars average selling price for some fairly unremarkable houses.

It is safe to say that Canadian home prices are out of wack in most large cities.

Just as in the United States, the "old economy" of heavy manufacturing is suffering up here too. General Motors is closing a huge plant in Oshawa, Ontario and laying off almost three thousand union auto workers. I was surprised to find out that Toyota, Honda, Ford, Chrysler, and GM all have large manufacturing operations in Ontario. The plant that is closing in Oshawa joins four that will be shuttered in the U.S. As Canada's largest partner, some of Trump's trade policies have many Canadians concerned. The general consensus here is that Canada needs to find other countries to trade with, especially in Asia and the Pacific, and not be so reliant on a very unpredictable U.S. administration in the future.

There are many versions of the "American Dream." The one to which I subscribed is that "anyone, if they are willing to work at it, can accomplish anything in the free American society." It was an excellent delusion for a few decades. I learned that there are some built-in limiting factors like race, religion, gender identity, and class that hinder many Americans from upward mobility. As a white man, I have very few limits. Yes, I was born into very humble circumstances, but, with education and life experience, I have advantages that many of my fellow citizens don't. Some call it "White Privilege," and many who benefit from it don't even know it exists.

My great friend, the Texas songwriter Eric Taylor sings about it in his classic folk-rock song *Deadwood South Dakota:*

"And the gold she lay cold in their pockets
And the sun she sets down on the trees
And they'll thank the Lord for this land that they live in
Where a white man, well, he does as he pleases…"

That's pretty much the rule. The white man, in this land called America, can pretty much do as he pleases.

That is until he has a medical emergency.

Over two-thirds of American bankruptcies are the result of unpaid medical bills. What most people fail to realize is that, even with medical insurance, many of the most routine medical procedures are not fully covered. I learned this first hand when my wife, who was paying $900 per month under the Affordable Care Act, or "ObamaCare," had a routine procedure and we got socked with an additional $5000 bill. And, before the hour-long procedure even began we had to pay the deductible amount upfront. I've worked as a nurse, and speak the medical jargon, but when I tried to find out exactly how much the out-patient visit was going to cost us, I couldn't get a straight answer. Neither the clinic or doctor's office nor the insurance company could give me a figure. I guess they make it up as they go along. Thankfully, we could afford it, but it was an unwelcome surprise. Like many other Americans, I thought the only out-of-pocket expense we'd have was the deductible. And, again, this was not some exotic operation; it was a routine preventive screening that millions of Americans had done every year. Considering that most working Americans can't come up with $400 cash for an emergency, this is alarming.

Which brings me to prison. I worked at some of the hardest prisons in America. As a traveling nurse contractor, I would provide my services to the institution in thirteen-week increments. If my work life was good, I'd renew; otherwise, I'd move on to another contract. It was the best of all worlds: I made great money, could work where and when I wanted to, and see much of the country. And, the one factor that allowed me to choose this type of work was that, as a result of my military career, my medical needs were covered by the Veteran's Administration. I am one of the lucky few who have 100% free medical coverage for life. (Or, at least as long as Trump doesn't blow up the V.A.

medical system). This medical safety net gave me a lot of freedom. I can't say the same for most of my colleagues working as the prison staff. For some reason, medical insurance in the U.S. is usually tied to one's employment. This was probably a good idea in 1957 when everyone who wanted to work at a company for life could, and it didn't take two jobs to equal one living wage. But now, when employers can't guarantee permanent, full-time hours, and there are few, if any, benefits, a job with medical insurance attached to it is valuable. But, this means that my prison co-workers were stuck. They often complained to me (and at me) that they utterly hated their jobs, but had to stay for the medical benefits. It made for some pretty miserable days behind bars - for the staff.

In Canada, medical insurance is provided by each province. There are taxpayer-funded insurance plans that cover almost everything. And, I know there are Americans who have been lied to by conservative talking heads, told that Canada's medical insurance is inadequate socialism, but they are wrong. By any measure, the routine and preventive medical care here in Canada is as good as anything in the United States. Of course, there is very little preventive care in the U.S. to speak of. But, in Canada, the preventive screenings and assessments lead to early detection of systemic conditions, and overall, a better health care experience. No, you are not going to get the province to pay for your breast or penis enhancement. Sorry. But, they will pay for your emergency heart bypass operation, and you will walk out of the hospital without stopping by the payment window. I've been to the hospital walk-in clinic with my wife twice, and I don't even know if there is such a thing as a payment window. Both times, she had her screenings done on time and walked away without worrying about how she would pay for them.

So, what does any of this have to do with the American Dream?

My argument is that because everyone has medical insurance, along with other components of the social safety net, people in Canada can be more entrepreneurial, more creative and more flexible in their careers. They can pursue their dreams. Ever wonder why there are so many great Canadian actors, musicians, and comedians on worldwide stages? It is because they have health insurance. A comic or musician can actually practice their art as a vocational career because they don't have to work at a restaurant or an Amazon shipping warehouse to cover medical insurance. If you are a nurse or guard working at a Canadian prison, and you choose to quit to pursue your dream of being a stand-up comic, you can do it because you aren't stuck at your miserable prison job in order to get some meager benefits package. Plus, believe it or not, you can get a lot of funny material from working at a prison. My most amusing stories come from the darkest places.

For many people, the American Dream is to live in a safe place. In my little Canadian town of 11,000, there is very little crime. Yeah, there are some petty things like shoplifting, public intoxication, reckless driving, and so on - but if you read the published police reports, most of the calls they get are for traffic issues or stray animals. Since I've been here, I have not seen or heard of a single violent crime in our community. The most serious thing lately was the overnight theft of some tools from a parked electrician's truck. I'd venture a guess that most police departments in the States wouldn't even investigate that one.

Yes, we leave our doors unlocked if we are not venturing very far. That, to me, is the type of peace of mind that contributes to my dream.

One of my goals as I sought my American Dream was to live in a small, friendly, Main Street town. I tried. I moved from several small American towns to others, looking for that vibrant little jewel of a place, but they all seemed to be on the way down. Empty storefronts, crumbling infrastructure, corrupt town management, you name it, these towns were snake bitten. In one Florida town, a small entrepreneurial group of gay men opened a restaurant, a few antique shops, and bed and breakfast. They were involved in many promising real estate ventures that would help revive the town. But, after a few years, the influential old-timers from the First Baptist Church ran them out of town by way of "gay boycotts" and sabotage. It was heartbreaking to see this. The B&B still sits empty and neglected, and the once posh restaurant has been demoted to the level of a greasy spoon diner. Some American Dream. Contrast that with my current small Canadian town. Last summer our town sponsored a gay pride parade and festival, even going so far as to fly the "Gay Rainbow" flag over the town hall for a week. This town is thriving, growing, and the kind of place I could only wish for in America.

Then, there is the subject of guns. Because it is damn near impossible to legally carry a firearm in Canada, the chances of me having an altercation on the street leading to gunshots fired is almost zero. For my huntin' lovin' outdoor American Bro's, I assure you, it is easy to buy a hunting rifle and take off into the woods to bag one of these giant Canadian white-tailed deer. It takes a bit of a background check and a safety course, and many Canadians own rifles and enjoy shooting sports. But, you aren't going down to the local outfitter's shop and quickly buy an AR-15 or any other military-type semi-automatic rifle. Military rifles are on the way to being illegal up here. The Liberal government has legislation in place to outlaw private ownership of military firearms. If you already have one, great, but it must be registered. When you die, your survivors must turn the weapon over to the police. Eventually, through attrition, only the police and army will have them, and that's it.

You may also notice that there are no school massacres in Canada. But, in all fairness, there have been some high profile shootings. In 2014 a mentally ill Montreal man, a fledgling terrorist, attacked the Canadian Parliament building, shooting and killing corporal Nathan Cirillo, who was standing ceremonial sentry duty near the War Memorial. The attacker was soon after shot and killed by the Parliamentary Sergeant-at-Arms, who first had to run to his office and retrieve his locked service weapon. However, as awful as this incident was, the shooter was armed with a .30-.30 Winchester lever-action hunting rifle - not exactly the preferred tool of terrorists. I owned the same firearm when I lived in Florida, and it has a capacity of eight rounds, and is very difficult to reload, especially on the fly in the field. If the Parliament Hill shooter had access to an AR-15 or AK-47, it could have been much worse.

Here's the bottom line: When I left the house in Florida, if I didn't have a handgun on my body, I felt vulnerable. When I leave the house in Canada, I feel entirely safe out in the wild world. After a few months living here, I stopped feeling naked without a gun. That is a big part of my American Dream; to live without the fear of being shot at for accidentally cutting someone off on the highway.

Then, there is my American Dream of living among wide-awake, kind, considerate people. America is known to be a loud, aggressive, competitive place. It seems that everyone is working a hustle, and I've worked a few of my own over the years. But, the older I got, the less interested I was in becoming the next Bill Gates or Michael Jordan. I accepted my limitations and did the best I could, regardless of the noise and distractions.

Canada is, on the other hand, a slower, kinder, more deliberate society. The word that always pops into my head is "consideration." There is a great effort made to be considerate of others up here, whether in traffic or a simple gesture like holding the door for someone at Tim Horton's coffee shop. Canadians seem to be aware that there are other people in the world, and the sun doesn't shine from their asses.

But, one thing I became more aware of was that, in general, over the past decade or so, there was a measurable dumbing down of the general American population. Maybe it's due to being medicated or under-educated, I don't know. People seemed less curious about the world, less interested in learning. For many, they turned to superstition and religion to explain the world around them. You only have to look at the subject of climate change to see how unscientific and delusional some Americans have become. Every season, there is more violent, unpredictable weather and each year more polar ice melts, resulting in sea level rise, flooding, and loss of coastal land. But, because Donald Trump told them that climate change is a Chinese hoax, they don't believe what hundreds of scientific experts have concluded as fact. Americans are applauding Trump for pulling out of the Paris climate accords and lifting EPA pollution regulations. Maybe they think Jesus will return to save them, but the last time I checked, he wasn't on duty at the weather station. I'm placing my bets with Bill Nye, the Science Guy.

Here in Canada, climate change is real. Perhaps because so much of Canada is located in the Arctic, there is no discussion, no debate about the ice fields melting due to human-made global warming. My wife, Jill, just finished production on a documentary film about the melting Arctic ice and how it affects the people and the wildlife of the North. She has seen it with her own eyes. She has witnessed the walrus, seals, whales and polar bears struggling to survive in the ever-warming climate. I suspect the closest President Trump has come to a polar bear is as a rug in someone's den. Jill has swum in the water, right next to them, studying the bears as they compete for a diminished food supply - due to global warming. I choose to believe her over The Donald.

I can't help but compare 2019 America to the society depicted in the great 2006 Mike Judge movie "Idiocracy." Do yourself a favor and watch it. Yes, it is over the top and absurd - for now.

So, again, I encourage you to get your passports up-to-date. Find a place in the world where you are your family can feel comfortable and look optimistically ahead to a prosperous future.

Life in the United States is about to take a nasty turn for a whole lot of very good people.

Hope Street

In 1965, when I was eight years old, our family moved into a modest row home on Hope Street in the Olney section of Philadelphia. Compared to the smaller house we left in a deteriorating North Philly neighborhood, it seemed like paradise. The new place had a front porch. There was a tiny back yard with a garage. We even had a patch of grass and a few flowers on the sloping front lawn. A big maple tree grew on the curb. I came to believe that my Dad intentionally chose to buy a house on "Hope Street" to plant a seed of optimism in my siblings and me.

Most of the other families on the street were much like ours. A mother, father, a gaggle of young kids and in a few cases, a dog or cat. A lot of the neighbors were just a generation or two "off the boat" from Ireland, Poland, Italy, and other European countries. Nineteen-sixties Philadelphia was buzzing with prosperity. Many of the men in Olney had served in World War Two. After returning to the States, they took advantage of the GI Bill to learn a trade or practice a profession. Anyone who wanted to work could. It was a promising time to be an American. Most families were comfortably supported with one income from their father's job. Some of the mothers stayed home and raised children. Other moms worked part-time. Rarely did a wife work full time if she had school-aged kids. I can't remember any single-parent families.

We children were being raised by the men who landed on the beaches at Normandy and the "Rosie the Riveter" women who kept the factories humming on the home front. These were the people that Tom Brokaw would later describe as "The Greatest Generation."

But the backgrounds of two specific Hope Street fathers were poles apart.

Alan Blumberg's Dad had a number tattoo' ed on his forearm, and Carl Schenk's father wore a deep scar across his cheek. Mr. Blumberg was a teenager when he was sent to a German concentration camp. Because he was a talented violinist, Blumberg was spared by the Nazi's and made to perform in the camp's Jewish orchestra. Mr. Schenk drove a German Panzer tank across the Polish border in the 1939 blitzkrieg. Soon after the invasion, Schenk defected to neutral Romania. We kids suspected that Mr. Schenk was still operating as a German spy. He had a lot of short-wave radio equipment and a big antenna mounted on his roof.

Despite their Dad's discordant histories, Jewish Alan and German Carl were great friends. They loved to hang out and put together model race cars. Alan had a very cool slot car racetrack on a platform in his basement. We would file down the steep cellar steps and watch as our friends raced their latest creations. I'll always remember the time that skinny Mr. Blumberg came downstairs to scold our little band of street urchins as the scale model racing got hot and our voices became louder and louder. In his heavily accented English, he chastised us saying "Hey you'se boys! My Alan play nice - why you'se boys no play nice like my Alan?"

That became something of a meme that poor Alan had to lug around until he graduated high school. "Hey, Alan, why you'se no play nice?"

Coming from a man who spent time in a Nazi concentration camp, and whose only child was best friends with the son of a German soldier, it seems like a reasonable appeal, even today. If only we contemporary Americans can get beyond our past disagreements and look ahead to an optimistic future for ourselves and our children, we may finally learn to "play nice."

Unfortunately, America has a long way to go. I watched with great heartache in the summer of 2017 as young

Americans flaunting Nazi symbolism marched through the Charlottesville, Virginia night carrying torches of hate. Dressed in golf shirts and tan khakis, (perhaps the whitest thing one can wear this side of a bedsheet and pointy hat with eye holes), they chanted abhorrent slogans meant to intimidate Blacks, Jews, and other American minorities. I couldn't help but wonder how many of these young white people had grandfathers who helped to liberate Europe from Hitler and the Third Reich. Was the grandchild of an American soldier who rescued Mr. Blumberg from a Nazi death camp now wearing a swastika armband on the hot streets of this Virginia college town?

The Alt-Right goon squad was met by the Antifa anarchists and violence ensued. American working-class foot soldiers from both the left and right engaged in skirmishes throughout the day. In the end, a vibrant young life was snuffed out. Heather Heyer, an innocent 32-year-old paralegal, and advocate for civil rights, came to her hometown to take a stand for equal justice. She was mowed down when a car driven by a white supremacist from Ohio was rammed into a crowd of counter-protestors. By that evening, five people were in critical condition, and a total of 35 protestors were seriously injured.

By now, President Trump's quote about the incident has taken on a life of its own. "You also had some very fine people on both sides," he said. I know it was blown out of context, and to be fair, he wasn't explicitly calling Neo-Nazis "fine people." But, in failing to condemn the alt-right instigators who organized the "Unite the Right" rally, he implied that they had his blessing. The net result of Trump's weak response and refusal to renounce the violent white supremacists was interpreted as a call to action for other racist white power groups and individuals. They realized that under the Trump administration, they would not be ostracized or investigated, and many white groups have developed a sense of empowerment. The "Proud Boys" are pretty certain that their guy sits in the oval office.

There are die-hard, radicalized people all over America who are just aching to be the spark that will light the next civil war. If and when Donald Trump is booted from office, either via impeachment or the 2020 election, they will rise up in numbers and intensity that will make Charlottesville seem like a genteel garden party.

At times I can't believe this is a real possibility in the America in which I was born and raised. There has always been a fringe element in the U.S. that threatened, (and practiced) political violence. But, today, the enmity is palpable, and the President of the United States is the catalyst. One need only read the alternative discussion forums online to gauge how the resentment and hatred are seething towards armed hostilities.

Here is a fairly typical posting, grammatical errors and all, from GodLike Productions, a Trump-friendly conspiracy forum:

June 19 2019 -

"If I were a low IQ Libtard, I would get used to the idea that Trump is winning a 2nd term. Whos going to stop him?

The weird thing this time around is the low IQ libturds are completely dalusional.

Absolutely impossible to have an intelligent converstion with one.

They are out of their minds (TDS) to the point of being dangerous psychopathic, homicidal lunatics.

I stay the hell away from them and when I am unfortunate enough to be in proximity to one of them, I am at 100% ready-to-go condition one carry status.

I believe most all of them suffer from demonic possession of some type or the delusion that God will allow them to fall into in the Last Days."

For those unfamiliar with the jargon of the far-right citizen's militias, "100% ready-to-go condition one status" is code for armed and ready with a live round in the gun's chamber, willing to shoot someone for the cause.

Of course (TDS) refers to the concept that all Liberals suffer from Trump Derangement Syndrome, and Donald Trump himself helped define it with this @realDonaldTrump tweet of July 18, 2018:

"Some people HATE the fact that I got along well with President Putin of Russia.
They would rather go to war than see this. It's called Trump Derangement Syndrome!"

The right uses phrases like this to imply that anyone who disagrees with Trump or his policies are in some way mentally incompetent and emotionally irrational. Trump's lack of self-awareness and use of projection is staggering. I used to think he did it intentionally, as a mechanism to gain advantage over his political foes, but after observing him for almost three years, I am convinced that Mr. Trump suffers from numerous psychological maladies. The unconscious transfer of his own character defects and intellectual shortcomings is just one of the psychiatric disorders he displays regularly. His Narcissistic Personality Disorder is perhaps the easiest abnormal behavior to observe because he could be the poster boy for the DSM-5[1] chapter on the subject. Here's what it has to say, in bullet format:

Persons with NPD usually display some or all of the following symptoms, typically without the commensurate qualities or accomplishments:

Grandiosity with expectations of superior treatment from other people

Fixation on fantasies of power, success, intelligence, attractiveness, etc.

Self-perception of being unique, superior, and associated with high-status people and institutions

Need for continual admiration from others

---

[1] Diagnostic Manual for Mental Health Practitioners

Sense of entitlement to special treatment and to obedience from others

Exploitation of others to achieve personal gain

Unwillingness to empathize with the feelings, wishes, and needs of other people

Intense envy of others, and the belief that others are equally envious of them

Constantly demeans, bullies and belittles others

Most patients only need to present with some of these characteristics to earn a diagnosis and treatment. I think The Donald runs the table. Again, this is only the most apparent mental disorder the President shows in public view. In my role as a nurse, I have worked with hundreds of people with behavioral and cognitive issues. Based on my experience, I suspect Donald Trump has a touch of early-onset dementia.

Dementia itself is not a specific disease but is usually associated with other behavioral and organic illnesses. His frequent lapses of memory, inability to recognize familiar people around him (Tim Apple, Rudy), deteriorating language skills (word salads), frequent long pauses and incoherent thought patterns when asked about simple White House policies, and his explosive emotional outbursts and mood changes, are all classic signs of dementia. He is a likely candidate for Borderline Personality Disorders, Sociopathy, and, depending on to whom you listen, maybe some Addiction issues. (Sex? Food? Stimulants like Adderall? Diet Coke?) Sorry, Evangelicals and Klansmen, your Dear Leader is a diagnosable loon.

Paraphrasing Nancy Pelosi, "someone in Trump's family or administration needs to perform an intervention."

I'm not holding my breath.

One of the many things that baffles me about the Trump presidency is how many Republican officials continue to support him. Most of the GOP officeholders are lawyers. They know the law. They know that Trump has broken dozens of them from the very first day he took office. They must know he is violating every trust and tradition of the presidency. They know there are checks and balances built into the Constitution to provide for a separation of powers amongst the three branches of the federal government. Yet, they do not challenge his lawlessness or question his competence. Now, as he prepares to run for reelection in 2020, Republicans, some who once vociferously opposed him, are kissing his ass and seeking his blessing as they seek to hold onto their seats in the halls of power.

Even those elected officials who are not lawyers know the basic difference between right and wrong. Yet, Trump, who more often than not, says or does the wrong thing for America if it is at odds with his personal business interests, is never taken to task by Republicans when he gives the finger to common decency and ethics.

At this point, the Democrats don't seem interested in impeachment. Armed with only the public findings of the Mueller Report, they have more than enough evidence to start a Judicial Committee inquiry. The Dems are playing politics instead of merely doing the right thing for the country. The Democratic leadership seems content to "run out the clock" on Trump's presidency, with the confidence that a Democratic candidate will defeat him in 2020.

They couldn't be more mistaken.

If Donald Trump makes it through to November of 2020, I have a strong feeling he will be re-elected. It will be a close contest, but he will be re-elected. And, sounding much like Trump during the 2016 campaign against Hillary Clinton, the losing side will claim the vote was rigged. They will be correct. I am suggesting that America get used to the fact that "free and fair" elections are a novelty of a bygone era.

I'm not claiming any psychic powers or special gifts, but I have also been having strong premonitions that Mike Pence will not be on the Trump 2020 ticket. That spot is most likely reserved for the spineless sycophantic Senator Lindsey Graham. It is the only theory that makes sense to explain Graham's complete 180-degree turn from one of Trump's most outspoken critics to one of his GOP lap dogs. Lindsey Graham has certainly sold his very soul to be just a heartbeat away from the presidency. Yes, it explains a lot.

Where will Putin be in all this 2020 drama? Winning. Winning bigly.

My father died when I was seventeen years old. One day he suddenly got sick in that house on Hope Street, and a few months later leukemia took him from us. A lot of my hope left with him. I hoped he would be with me as I became a man and learned about the world. I hoped he would be around to help me form my ideas and opinions. I hoped he'd lend guidance as I navigated the complex requirements of the twenty-first century. I hoped he would share my happiness when I met and married Jill, my soul mate and love of my life.

But, in the short time he was with us, one of the most important things Dad instilled in my sisters and me is a sense of justice and fair play. My Dad also taught us about our responsibilities as citizens. Dad would gather us on election day, and we'd walk up the street with him to the polling place on the corner. We'd wait outside the little deli across the street, and volunteers would give us candy and campaign stickers. He always stressed that in addition to our Rights, we also had Responsibilities. Our little trips to Olde City Philadelphia always included a U.S. history lesson that was heavy on the ethics of democracy. He purposely had us walk in the footsteps of the Founders because he wanted to imprint in us how unique this experiment called America is among the history of all nations in the world. He'd be heartbroken that the noble experiment may soon fail.

But still, there is some hope. Our democracy depends on wide-awake young people. The next generation must be prepared to reboot the entire system!

If America is to continue as the beacon of freedom and justice in the world, it will be the Millenial and Gen-Z digital generations who will have to step up and replace the old white guys in ties. I am 62 years old, just a bit younger than the average age of all sitting U.S. Senators, but there are many Senators and Representatives, as well as Cabinet Secretaries who are well into their eighties. The country that the wrinkled old doddering puss's in Washington is leaving for the next few generations needs triage. It is time for a youth movement in American politics. Their

American Dream has been reduced to paying off student loans and finding meaning in underpaid work. The younger American generations must wrestle control of this nation from the grasp of the corrupt power brokers by any means necessary. Let me be clear: By. Any. Means. Necessary.

They must tear down the corrupt patriarchy that lords over them and replace it with an honest, legitimate, transparent system. They must build a new Great Society that includes everyone, especially minorities and women. Women are 51% of the U.S. population, yet only hold 25% of Senate seats. Twenty-five women are serving in the United States Senate, 17 Democrats and 8 Republicans. Although there are a record number of female Members serving in the House of Representatives, they still only make up 23% of the total voting seats. I've always subscribed to the philosophy that women make better decisions than men, can work collaboratively, and have an intrinsic sense of fair play. And, many of them are moms. Mothers with children should be the most honored and celebrated members of society. How they do it, I don't know. I don't have a parental bone in my body, and it amazes me when I see young moms raising children, managing a household, working an outside job, and juggling the family finances. If they can do this, they certainly can be my elected representative.

At this point in my life, my hope for America is of indirect consequence. I've made my decision to leave. I am well on my way to completing all the requirements for Canadian immigration. My dreams for America are dreams for my sisters and brothers. I've invested blood and treasure in the campaign to make the United States a gentler, kinder, more peaceful, and positive place to thrive. But, people like me, who cared about each other and wanted a just society, were outgunned and outspent by hateful, greedy, corrupt men and women who now are sailing the Ship of State precariously close to the rocks. They don't give a flying shit-in-the-air about the fate of average working Americans because they've all got mega-yacht lifeboats standing by at the ready. They will sip fine whiskey and laugh as they watch you in steerage class clawing at the locked hatches as you sink to the bottom and drown.

We can only hope our children are better navigators of these chaotic stormy seas.

Independence Day

It is a weird coincidence that I am about to finish writing this book on July 4th, American Independence Day. I've been traveling in support of one of Jill's media projects for about three weeks, so I put this writing venture aside for a bit. We drove and camped all across the Canadian maritime provinces. The breathtaking natural beauty and remarkably kind people of Quebec, Prince Edward Island, Nova Scotia, New Brunswick, and Newfoundland have been a pleasant distraction from the turmoil surrounding Trump and everything he touches. We were too busy, wholly engaged in the wonder of the remarkable moments before us, to waste much headspace thinking about Donald "Fucking" Trump.

Yes, our Newfoundland friends and colleagues asked me, the sole American in our group, "what the hell is going on down there?" Over and again, they expressed confusion and deep concern about the current state of affairs in "The States." And, to a person, every one of these Canadians vowed that they would not travel to the United States as long as Trump is president. These are some of the top people working in the outdoor adventure industry, making documentary films, publishing magazines, and traveling the world for a living. They are turning down assignments and jobs if it entails travel to the U.S. They concede that they will likely suffer some mild financial pain, but their personal morals and ethics prevent them from betraying their standards. And it is a two-way street. The American businesses they would normally patronize, including airlines, lodging, and logistics, are going to suffer because a large group of Canadians are choosing to stay away. I wonder if the Trump administration even considers the damage he has done to the economy because thousands of people the world over refuse to come to the United States while it is governed by his criminal regime. (Some economist Ph.D. candidate should measure this.)

And, I don't use the word "regime" lightly. Trump is the tyrant sitting atop an authoritarian government that looks a lot like the crooked system that brought down the former Soviet Union. It doesn't take a psychologist to see that he admires strongmen and dictators. Even today, the birthday of American freedom and independence, he displays all the trappings of a third world despot. Trump has hijacked the annual Washington D.C. Independence Day celebration and tried to make it all about him. His infatuation with the military trappings of power and oppression has him demanding that the U.S. Army roll tanks onto the streets of D.C. so he can look like a strong leader. Everyone with half a brain knows that such displays are nothing more than overcompensation for insecurity and weakness. But, it must make his little mushroom dick hard to see the tanks, smell the diesel, and hear the jets roaring overhead as he waves from his golden throne in front of the Lincoln memorial. Poor Abe is rolling in his grave, saying, "if I have to listen to a speech by this stable genius, please shoot me again."

In my time as a Staff Sergeant in the U.S. Army National Guard, I was in charge of the medical platoon of an armored battalion. We had M1 Abrams tanks and an assortment of other tracked vehicles to support the tanker's mission. As a person who has witnessed up-close and personal the devastation a main battle tank can mete out, I understand why American citizens are wary of tanks on their streets. More than their firepower, however, is the message they convey. Whoever commands the tanks controls the psychological battlefield. The people of D.C. don't want their streets used to send King Trump's message. In other dictatorships, North Korea and Russia for example, the tanks are paraded in the capitol as a message to the masses: "We can destroy you, so stay in line and be obedient." To whom is Trump sending his message? He is trying to communicate not to sovereign nations who may engage us, but to his domestic political opponents. It is all a reality show where appearances mean everything.

(By the way, the only time we off-loaded our armor in a U.S. city was after Hurricane Katrina. We didn't bring M1 battle tanks; we brought our M113 tracked ambulances so we could rescue and evacuate people from the muddy, flooded Mississippi Delta.)

America's march towards fascism is happening at a frightening pace. I am sinking into mild depression every time I read my Twitter feed or watch a cable news program. I am actually measuring how much Trump news I consume each day because I really believe it is affecting my mood and mental state. As each day passes and I see that there is little opposition to the authoritarian lawlessness of the president, I become more despondent. Don't people know that supporting Trump will lead to a complete collapse of American democracy as we know it? It really is nothing short of a constitutional emergency, yet many Americans are far more concerned about which pronouns to use and boycotting Nike shoes over a Betsy Ross flag. For fuck's sake, people! Wake up!

In 2007, nine years before Trump was elected president, Rhodes Scholar and activist author Naomi Wolf published "The End of America." In it, she outlined the ten steps towards fascism:

#1. Invoke a terrifying internal and external enemy

#2. Create secret prisons where torture takes place

#3. Develop a thug caste or paramilitary force not answerable to citizens

#4. Set up an internal surveillance system

#5. Infiltrate and harass citizen's groups

#6. Engage in arbitrary detention and release

#7. Target key individuals

#8. Control the press

#9. Cast criticism as espionage and dissent as treason

#10. Subvert the rule of law

Choose your own examples and fill in the blanks using a typical day in Trump's America.

I'm going to focus on just a few points -

#1: Trump has invoked Muslims, Iranians, brown people of all Latin American nationalities, MS-13, progressive liberals, and the free press as enemies of America.

#2: Gitmo. The border immigration detention camps.

#3: Trump lauds his Bikers, Proud Boys, Neo-Nazis; all his "tough guys."

#8: Fox News. Trump's propaganda machine.

#9. Count how many times Trump calls the press, his political opponents, federal officials who opposed him, (James Comey, for example) and a former African-American president treasonous. And of course, "Lock her up!"

#10. Law? What law? "Fuck your congressional subpoenas and lower court judge's rulings!"

It is a mere stone's throw from fascism to genocide and ethnic cleansing.

According to Dr. Gregory H. Stanton,[2] here are the 10 steps to Genocide, with my commentary:

#1. Classification - "Us and them." Pretty much Trump's approach to everything, foreign or domestic.

#2. Symbolization - Swastikas, MS-13, MAGA. Breaking every group down to its simple tribal images. This goes for "both sides."

---

[2] Genocide Studies, George Mason University

#3. Discrimination - Trump's group of powerful white people deny basic rights to minorities, be they brown, black, or women.

#4.Dehumanization - Contractor prison guards make detained immigrants drink from toilets, like dogs. It is easy to be brutal once the personhood is stripped away.

#5.Organization - Usually by the State. I said from the beginning that Trump's ICE agents would hide behind badges and guns to do his dirtiest of state-sponsored dirty work.

#6. Polarization - Extremist groups become the norm. Moderates are ostracized, shunned, arrested. The GOP Congressman who called for Trump's impeachment will be one of the first.

#7. Preparation - The MAGA Militias who support Trump are arming up, ready to "purify" the white nation on his command. At first, they cloak their true intentions - but then justify murder with "if we don't kill them, they will kill us!"

#8. Persecution - Gathering up "illegals" and corralling them into camps and denying children basic sanitation, toothbrushes, medical care. Forcibly taking children from parents. This list of despicable examples is very long. Just read the news each day.

#9. Extermination - Trump is almost here, but not quite. I think the only thing holding him back is his ambition to be reelected. Even (some) of his base will object if he starts to casually kill brown people. I'll quote Dr. Stanton: "(Extermination)...quickly becomes the mass killing legally called genocide. It is extermination to the killers because they do not believe their victims to be fully human. When the state sponsors it, the armed forces often work with militias to do the killing. Sometimes the genocide results in revenge killings by groups against each other, creating the downward whirlpool-like cycle of bilateral genocide... Acts of genocide demonstrate how dehumanized the victims have become. Already dead bodies are dismembered; rape is used as a tool of war to genetically alter and eradicate the other group. Destruction of cultural and religious property is employed to annihilate the group's existence from history..."

#10. Denial - the perpetrators hide the evidence, deny involvement, obstruct investigations, destroy records, intimidate witnesses, blame it on the victims.

Any of this sound familiar?

The United States of America under Trump is one unlawful executive order away from exterminating the thousands of Latin American refugees who came to the border seeking asylum. Rather than detaining and processing them, the goons with the guns and badges may find it expeditious to dispatch them with extreme prejudice. The ICE agents and contractors are just a wink-and-a-nod away from digging trenches behind the camps and eliminating Trump's immigrant problem. It would be Trump's final solution to his self-inflicted crisis.

There are tanks in the nation's capital and concentration camps at its border.

Happy 4th of July!

I Still Have a Dream

Between watching my birth country fall apart and getting settled into my new one, it has been a stressful year. It seems as though every few days brings on more worrisome political developments down south. The constant chaos emanating from the White House, the scandals, lawlessness and wiping their butts with the Constitution is the standard operating procedure for this administration. Somehow, this dysfunction has been normalized. I guess anything short of a full-scale planetary crisis each day is a win for humanity. Like many others, I expected that the institutions that historically shored up the bulwarks of American society would prevail over a rogue president and his collaborators.

I was wrong.

My eyes are now wide open to reality. Donald Trump will not be indicted; he will not be removed from power by Congress or through some last-ditch effort that invokes the 25th amendment. He will continue on the authoritative, destructive trail he has blazed for more than two years. His power has been consolidated, and he is the most dangerous threat to American democracy today. I'm freaked out. I've been on edge for months, waiting for Nancy Pelosi or Robert Mueller to bring down the curtain on Trump's shit show, but they have done little to make me feel any better. Now I'm fearful he's going to have an encore.

Congress is impotent. The Press is neutered. The Courts are stacked with cronies. The military is perplexed. The balance of power in Washington has shifted in favor of Trump and his unethical allies. The federal government of the United States has been commandeered by a bunch of immoral pirates, yet the American public seems more concerned about a little brown actress playing the part of a Disney mermaid. I believe the election of Donald Trump brought out the worst in society. People who would have hidden their racism and xenophobia are following Trump's lead and putting it on public display. For most of my life, no matter the party or political philosophy, the President was a man to be respected. Now, the President of the United States is the negative example we point to when illustrating a general lack of ethics. Donald Trump is not the type of guy you'd want your child to admire. He is a carnival barker and reality show promoter. How did the most insecure person in our country (who has to pay porn stars to have sex with him) rise to such powerful heights? How did a shady New York businessman who managed to bankrupt a casino, become the person with the most influence over the world's economy? How did a self-described stable genius, who can't form a sentence without lying, become the leader of the free world? Because he represents precisely who America is. He is what America has become; An Idiocracy in the hands of hustlers and swindlers of all stripes.

From an Attorney General who is shielding this president from investigations and prosecution to an EPA administrator who seems hell-bent on destroying what's left of the fragile environment, Trump has stacked his cabinet with lapdogs and boot-lickers. Is it un-American for me to criticize the president? Or to say that there are corrupt criminals, loyal only to Trump installed in every important American institution? No, it is the most America thing I can do - speak truth to power and hope there are enough good people remaining engaged in the American political process to resurrect the lofty ideals set forth by Jefferson and Washington. Those convictions and principles should not be forgotten.

There is one thing for which we can thank Donald Trump. He has flushed everything out into the open. Every vile character defect bubbling under the surface of the American political discourse has now been laid bare. From the Republican enablers in the Senate to the tiki-torch marchers in Charlottesville, we can clearly see what he and his fervent followers represent. The question I present today is, "How much longer will average working Americans tolerate Trump's lies, blatant criminality, and incompetence?"

It is now time for all of us to choose America's destiny. We are at the tipping point that will decide our children's futures. The political, economic, and environmental ramifications of our decisions today will determine if humanity survives as a species. Sorry to be the bearer of bad news, but there are no reserved seats for you and me on Elon Musk's rockets to Mars.

In last week's mail, I received my U.S. voter registration card so that I can vote absentee from Canada. I can't blame you for feeling that your vote won't count, but I am certain there are millions of good people in America who care about the future as much as I do. The political process has been gerrymandered and rigged against so many of us that it may seem futile even to show up. But this election is different. If Trump wins another term, there will be no stopping the right-wing thugs in the streets or the criminal despots in government. We must vote Trump out so overwhelmingly that there can not be a single state in which he has a chance to challenge the results successfully. And, we must send a clear signal that if he refuses to peacefully transition executive power to the newly-elected president, he will have little popular support. I would, however, enjoy seeing him frog-marched out of the oval office by a squad of female U.S. Marshals.

I will borrow from my Canadian wife's strategic reserve of optimism. If we vote with our ballots and wallets in resounding unity, we have one last chance to rescue American democracy and see it preserved.

My American dream is that you and your loved ones can live a peaceful, prosperous, fulfilling life in the country whose people I will always love as my brothers and sisters.

Epilogue

I am a survivor. I have been at a crossroads many times in my life. Decisions I make are always motivated by my desire to move forward through an extraordinary life experience. There is never a single day that I take for granted. When relationships, employment, or living conditions become dysfunctional, I don't wait for them to become a crisis. I know when it is time to leave. I walk away.

My mother still wonders why I left my first "real" job as a production manager at a big concert company. She's convinced I'd be rich and famous, if I'd stayed with them. She ignores the part where half of the management staff were dealing cocaine and the other half were laundering money for the Philly mob. (Fortunately, the federal indictments stopped just above my pay grade.)

There were many instances where I could have settled in to a cushy career with advancement opportunities and significant compensation. I tried that route a few times and it was a terrible fit. The key word was always "settle." I have never settled for anything. I am always looking over the hill and around the corner for the next remarkable experience. A psychologist friend has classified Jill and me as "novelty and sensation seekers." I'll accept that. We are both the kind of people who need constant physical, intellectual and spiritual stimulation to feel fulfilled and alive.

The current situation in the United States has reached a critical point. Without some quick and extreme course corrections, American society will implode. There will be political, cultural, and economic convulsions unlike any experienced in modern times. I've studied history and comprehend man's potential for inhumane behavior. One only has to look at the Trump Administration's treatment of immigrants legally seeking asylum at the southern border to predict how this cruel, sadistic script plays out. I don't think anyone except perhaps Trump's immediate family is immune to his ruthless brutality. Just because you are wearing your red MAGA hat and feel empowered by his demagoguery, don't think that you won't fall victim to Trump's complete dismantling of the American Dream.

I'm not hanging around for the worst-case scenarios to be realized.

I am a survivor.

Social Links:

Robert frequently creates content on YouTube.
Please watch, share, and subscribe at:
www.YouTube.com/RobertMcClellanNetwork

Robert rants on Twitter almost every day.
Please follow: @McClellanRobert

Against his better judgement, Robert has a mediocre Facebook page. It is sometimes the only way he can keep up with his wife, the acclaimed underwater explorer, author, and filmmaker, Jill Heinerth.

He needs friends, please:
www.FaceBook.com/RobertMcClellanWriter
Jill's Facebook is much more interesting at:
www.FaceBook.com/JillHeinerth

Both Robert and Jill are online with Podcasts, Blogs, Images and other cool content at:

www.IntoThePlanet.com

www.RobertMcClellan.com

If you are thinking of moving to Canada, there is more information at:

https://www.canada.ca/en/services/immigration-citizenship.html

Biography

Robert McClellan is an acclaimed writer, editor, and media expert. He combines a lifetime of creative dexterity with a resourceful, contemporary skill set.

An early Internet enthusiast, Robert has a number of professional podcasts and blogs to his credit. He created and hosts the popular "Real Sobriety Podcast" and is Producer/Co-Host of the "Into the Planet Podcast with Jill Heinerth." He wrote, produced, and appears in the award-winning documentary films "Real Sobriety," and "Ben's Vortex." He is the co-creator of the environmental call to action, "We Are Water Project." His first book, "Boom Baby Boom" is available on Amazon. Robert's latest project is "Leaving Trump's America", a book, podcast, and video series about moving to Canada in the wake of Donald Trump's authoritarian rise to power.

Robert's views of the world demand that we give each other room to live free, yet take care of others who need help. His unique social perspective was formed on the working class streets of Philadelphia, where sometimes, the most effective charitable act included an educational punch in the nose.

An unapologetic novelty-seeker, Robert has had more than a handful of interesting livelihoods; Navy combat photographer, Army field medic, live concert production manager, radio talk show host, truck driver, prison nurse, writer, filmmaker, and podcaster.

Avid cyclists, Robert and his wife, the acclaimed underwater explorer, author, and filmmaker Jill Heinerth, rode over 7000 km across Canada to search for their perfect home. In 2018, they moved to Jill's birth country, taking up residence in a quiet bicycle-friendly community. As Creative Director of Heinerth Productions, Inc., Robert explores his boundaries every day. Whether it is a new documentary film idea or a book project, he embraces the opportunity to create something that he can be proud of, that will resonate with people around the world.

Made in the USA
Middletown, DE
28 July 2019